Himalayan Cats

The moral rights of the author has been asserted
British Library Cataloguing in Publication Data
A catalogue record for this book is available from the British Library

ISBN 978-1-909820-41-8

Disclaimer and Legal Notice

While every attempt has been made to verify the information shared in this publication, neither shall the author nor publisher assume any responsibility for errors, omissions, nor contrary interpretation of the subject matter herein. Any perceived slight to any specific person(s) or organisation(s) are purely unintentional. You need to do your own due diligence to determine if the content of this product is correct for you.

This book is presented solely for educational and entertainment purposes. The author and publisher are not offering it as legal, accounting, or other professional services advice. While best efforts have been used in preparing this book, the author and publisher make no representations or warranties of any kind and assume no liabilities of any kind with respect to the accuracy or completeness of the contents and specifically disclaim any implied warranties of merchantability or fitness of use for a particular purpose. Neither shall the author nor the publisher be held liable or responsible to any person or entity with respect to any loss or incidental or consequential damages caused, or alleged to have been caused, directly or indirectly, by the information or programs contained herein. The author shall not be liable for any loss incurred as a consequence of the use and application, direct or indirectly, of any information presented in this work. This publication is designed to provide information in regard to the subject matter covered. It is the reader's responsibility to find advice before putting anything written in the book into practice.

References are provided for informational purposes only and do not constitute endorsement of any websites or other sources. Readers should be aware that the websites listed in this book may change. We have no control over the nature, content, and availability of the websites listed in this book. The inclusion of any website links does not necessarily imply a recommendation or endorse the views expressed within them. EKL Publishing takes no responsibility for, and will not be liable for, the website being temporally unavailable or being removed from the internet. The information in this book is not intended to serve as legal advice.

Himalayan Cats

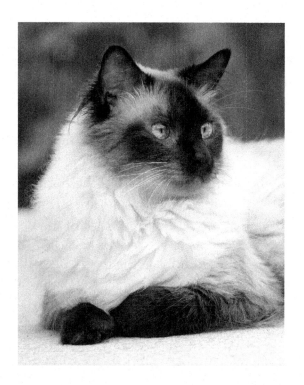

**The Complete Owner's Guide to
Himalayan Cats and Kittens**
*Including Buying, Daily Care, Personality,
Temperament, Health, Diet and Breeders*

Colette Anderson

Foreword

The Himalayan is one of my favorite cats because these longhaired beauties are a mixture of two superb breeds, the Persian and the Siamese.

I've lived with both of the foundation breeds. The Siamese is a completely unique and forceful little soul. They are insanely intelligent, driven to communicate, and determined to manage every aspect of your life.

Mine was a regular little drill sergeant, holding me to my schedule with rigid dedication and fussing at me with annoyed yowls when I deviated from the norm. Most people don't realize that Siamese cats are strong. Mine could literally push me out of "his" side of the bed.

Persians, on the other hand, are the living definition of mellow. Sweet faced and soft of voice, a Persian is affectionate but patient, happy to sit and wait for your time and attention. "Wait" is not in the vocabulary of a Siamese!

So what happens when you put these two breeds together? Frankly, it's the best of both worlds! The first time I saw a Himalayan, I was captivated. They have the beautiful color points of the Siamese with the gorgeous long fur and round curves of the Persian.

Himalayans are as intelligent and interactive as the Siamese, but as patient and soft-spoken as the Persian. They are excellent companions for singles or families, and don't suffer from the kind of separation anxiety evident in so many of the Oriental breeds.

My initial hesitation over owning another longhaired breed settled down immediately when I realized how cooperative Himalayans are by nature. It's really not a chore to spend 10-15 minutes a day brushing a cat when the cat cooperates!

As a dedicated ailurophile, which sounds so much better than "crazy cat lady," there really are few felines I've ever met that I didn't fall in love with immediately.

It's hard not to fall in love with a Himalayan. Technically, we're talking about a blue-eyed pointed Persian, but that dash of Siamese blood infuses the Himalayan with just that little something "extra" that makes the Himmie a distinct and distinctly wonderful breed.

Acknowledgments

I would like to thank and dedicate this book to my mother Rosemarie for her love and encouragement down through the years and for instilling in me my love for all animals but especially cats.

To my wonderful husband Nick, thank you again for all your help and assistance and for undertaking the dreaded proof reading. His observations and comments are as always invaluable.

Just a note to say that I have written this book using American spelling as that is what I'm used to. I have given measurements in both feet and inches/pounds and ounces and also in metric. I have also given costs in US$ and GBP. Both the measurements and costs are approximate guides. I have done my best to ensure the accuracy of the information in this book as at the time of publication.

Table of Contents

Chapter 1 – Introduction

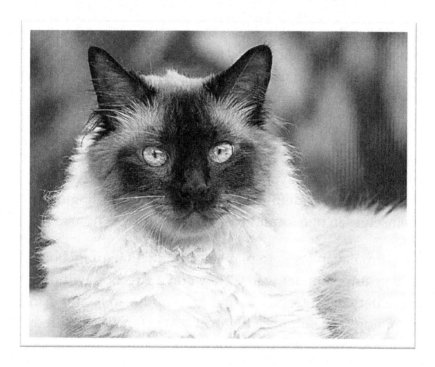

The cat we know as the "Himalayan" is really an especially lovely form of the Persian. In fact, in Europe these cats are called "Himalayan Persians" or "Colorpoint Persians."

The sub-breed was created by crossing the Persian with the Siamese to cultivate beautiful long-haired cats with consistently blue eyes and darker "points" at the feet, ears, tail and face.

For this reason, the Himalayan's history is identical to that of the Persian. For the most part these cats have the calm, gentle, and unflappable demeanor of the Persian breed rather than the more demanding, relentlessly attention-seeking, vocal attitude of the powerhouse Siamese.

Some Himalayans will have a longer more oriental conformation to their bodies as opposed to the cobby, short-legged stockiness of the typical Persian, but this is not the preferred conformation for show cats.

The mix with the Siamese has created a sub-breed that is highly intelligent, sweet tempered, social, and an excellent companion. Himalayans also tend to be more active than Persians who are definitely prone to artfully arranging themselves in one location and staying put for hours.

The Himalayan loves to play fetch and will happily bound after crumped paper wads. They crave affection without being demanding, and are highly receptive to lap time and grooming. The latter is a huge advantage in a longhaired cat whose coat needs daily attention

History of the Persian Breed

The modern Persian from which the Himalayan sprang came into existence through a century and a half of careful breeding by enthusiasts. The goal was to create a companion animal that was both elegant and exceptionally personable.

Since Persians are universally recognized as one of the most popular and elegant of all cat breeds, these efforts were unusually successful. It is not, however, easy to say exactly when the first Persians reached Europe.

There are multiple reports of diplomats returning to Europe and England from postings in Asia in the 1800s accompanied by longhaired cats. These animals were referred to by their place of origin. Cats from Iran or Persia thus became "Persians."

One of the earliest verifiable references to such longhaired cats was made by the renowned traveler Pietro della Valle in the 1600s. In his travelogue, "Voyages de Pietro della Valle," there are descriptions of longhaired cats from the Khorazan province of Persia that were transported to India by Portuguese sailors.

There are even earlier reports of such cats coming to Europe in the 1300s in the care of returning Crusaders. It is safe to say that these exotic cats were crossbred to the shorthaired street cats of Europe, contributing genes to existing well-loved breeds like the modern British Shorthair.

But the purity of the longhaired line was also protected when many of the animals become the preferred pets of royalty, especially in the French court. In England, Queen Victoria kept two blue Persians.

The modern Persian breed was really fostered into existence in the United Kingdom where cat fanciers developed breeding programs to refine the most desirable characteristics of the modern breed.

At the first cat show held at the Crystal Palace in London in 1871, Persians were prominently displayed. Since that time the Persian line has been distinguished by highly specific stocky, large-boned body conformation.

Persians have pleasingly rounded heads topped by small ears. The eyes are round and sweet, and the noses are short and "smushed."

The Persian breed was brought to the United States early in the 20th century, and has grown wildly in popularity since. It was in the U.S.A. in the 1930s that the real work of crossing the Persian and Siamese lines began.

Cultivating the Persian / Siamese Cross

While efforts were underway in the United States to develop the Persian / Siamese cross that we know today as the Himalayan, independent efforts were begun in the UK by Brian Sterling Webb.

In 1955, the Governing Council of the Cat Fancy recognized the Longhaired Colorpoint. The breed received recognition by the Cat Fanciers Association in the U.S. in 1957 as the Himalayan. Since that time, more than 343,000 Himalayans have been registered in the U.S.A. alone.

The breeders were originally interested in achieving a longhaired variant of the classic Siamese coloration, but also concentrated on retaining the best qualities of the Persian.

Consequently, Persian genes continued to be introduced into the Himalayan line into the 1980s to prevent the cats from having longer, sleeker bodies and smaller heads.

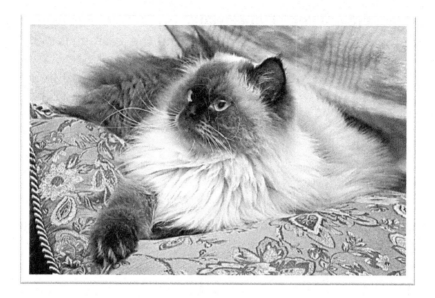

Physical Characteristics

These efforts successfully retained the rounded, cobby Persian body in the Himalayan, which today is a short-legged cat, with little inclination to jump.

Like Persians, Himalayans are medium-sized cats that typically weigh 7-12 pounds / 3.17-5.44 kg. They have long, thick coats that fall elegantly over their bodies, forming a ruff at the neck.

Their tails are short, straight, and heavily plumed. A well-groomed Himalayan coat is silky and smooth to the touch. The hair is so dense it has the texture of fine velvet.

The eyes should be round and large while the nose is small and may appear flat or normal. The ears tilt slightly forward and are generously studded with hair at the base.

It is not unusual for a Himalayan queen to have a large litter of kittens – as many as 12-14 – but the average is 3-5.

Himalayans have a lifespan of 10-18 years, with most living past 15 years.

Colorations

The Himalayan was officially recognized in seal, blue, chocolate, and lilac points in 1957, followed by flame and tortie points in 1964. Cream points were added in 1979, and lynx in 1982.

The seal point is the most basic coloration for the Himalayan, and is the expression of a gene for black points. If an agouti tabby gene is added, the result is a Seal Lynx Point, which is best described as black "painted" or highlighted points.

Although chocolate and lilac points are among the oldest recognized colorations, both are difficult to achieve due to complex genetics involving recessing genes.

Chocolate is a dominant color, but is recessive to black, so a cat must have two copies of the chocolate gene to exhibit the chocolate point. If there is also an agouti tabby gene is the genetic mix, you will get a Chocolate Lynx Point. Lilac is a dilute of chocolate and also requires two copies of the gene.

Flame and tortie points are much easier to breed and are highly popular because of the striking contrasts they create. Flame is an expression of a red gene, which presents a stark counterpoint to the cat's pure white coat. Torties are a gorgeously mottled combination of black and red.

Cream and blue-cream points are dilutions of the flame and tortie colorations. The lynx points, which are striped or tabby patterned, are highly sought after and, as discussed above, can occur in combination with any of the other colors.

The Personality of the "Himmie"

Himalayans are not hyperactive, but they do like to play a bit more than other Persians. When they're done, however, they're quite happy to have some lap time. True to their Siamese genes, however, Himmies are "supervisors," and will be right there with you, participating in the activity at hand.

These are the kinds of cats who will "help" you read the newspaper, and stick their heads up under your book in bed. In the process of supervision, they will comment and offer advice, but they have sweet, melodious voices and seem thoroughly genuine in their efforts to communicate.

A Siamese might "say" the same of himself, but I've always had the vague feeling that the venerable cat of the Orient fancies he knows my business much better than I do!

Male or Female?

The "male or female" question is fairly standard, but with the Himalayan it really doesn't matter. Both genders are equally personable and easy going. I've seen little difference in personality based on gender.

In general, I'm much more prone to take cats on an individual basis and to consider the factor of environment in the development of temperament.

Like all cats with Persian genes, Himmies are calm and even-tempered. However, the breed also derives its independent streak from its Siamese antecedents. The result is a cat that knows its own mind, but is quite pleasant about getting what it wants.

Some people shy away from males of any breed due to the potential for urine spraying, but I don't see this as a problem. I have never had a tom that sprayed in the house. The behavior is extremely rare with neutered males and has been, in my opinion, blown out of proportion.

More than One?

There is absolutely nothing to prevent anyone from having multiple Himalayans. They are quite companionable with one another, and a pair of Himmies will certainly keep one another company while you're off at work.

The only caution I would raise is that two longhaired cats take twice the time for daily grooming. Combing out a

Himmie requires 5-15 minutes, and you will also need professional grooming for your pet about once a month. Two Himmies equal twice the cost at the kitty "spa."

With Other Pets

Himalayans tend to "room" quite well with other pets, even dogs, so long as the other animals are well behaved. No Himmie is going to like being constantly harassed by a dog, and although these are truly sweet cats, they still have Siamese genes and will raise paw and claw to put Fido in his place.

As for other types of pets, Himalayans, as obvious as it may be to say so, are cats. They might not dive into the fish tank or make a real effort to climb up to the budgie's cage, but if given a chance, instinct may take over.

All multi-species households would do well to follow a policy of benign segregation with securely latched cages and tight fitting lids to protect those pets that are, in a cat's eyes, "prey."

With Children

Himalayans are certainly not contentious cats, and they integrate nicely into families, but their preference is certainly for children with good manners.

For those most part a Himmie will just remove himself from the scene if the kids are getting to be too much. I do strongly advocate that children be taught from an early age to respect animals of all kinds and to deal with them gently and respectfully.

I'm afraid I always come down on the side of the cat first. If a pet is being handled roughly or harassed, it's simply in the cat's nature to react if he cannot remove himself. It seems to me that the question should be, who needs to be admonished, the cat or the child?

Inside or Out?

Obviously a pedigreed cat like a Himalayan is an expensive investment. Also, longhaired cats do not make good outside cats because exposure to the elements and vegetation greatly complicates caring for their coats.

Beyond those considerations, however, I do not believe any cat, including the very hardy Domestic Shorthair, often referred to as an "alley cat," should be allowed outside.

My cats have been exclusively indoor pets for the more than 40 years that I have had feline companions. I do not believe they have suffered any deprivation, and, in fact, have benefited enormously. Many of my pets have lived well in excess of 15 years regardless of breed.

Our modern world is a dangerous place for our beloved animal companions. Whether that danger arises from automobiles, aggressive dogs, wildlife, or bad humans, the risk is not worth it in my opinion. I would never dream of allowing my cats access to the outside world.

There are many cat owners who achieve a compromise position by designing some kind of secure enclosed structure that allows their cats to be contained while enjoying sunlight and fresh air and the sounds of the outside world.

I have done this with my pets, and so long as you can securely bring your cat in and out of the structure, I think this is an excellent idea. There are no set designs for these kinds of enclosures, but you can easily find many good ideas online through your favorite search engine.

"Himmie" Pros and Cons

Assembling a set of "pros" and "cons" associated with any type of animal is not as simple as some people think. These things are very much a matter of personal perception.

I was raised around dogs and am very fond of them, but I have no desire to keep a dog as a pet because I don't want to have to walk one. Other people think the walks are absolutely the best part of dog ownership.

Himalayans are fantastic cats with the perfect mix of agreeable Persian and intelligent, independent Siamese blood. They are affectionate and interactive, adapting well to your schedule and not suffering from separation anxiety. They will be there at the end of the day to welcome you home from work, but unlike a pure Siamese, they won't spend the day serenading the neighbors with lonely yowls.

Frankly, the biggest argument against having any longhaired cat is the need for daily grooming augmented with professional grooming sessions. This means a daily time commitment and some additional monthly expense. If those things draw you up short, consider a shorthaired cat. Otherwise, the Himalayan is an excellent companion animal both in its physical conformation and its native disposition.

Chapter 2 – Adopting Your Himalayan

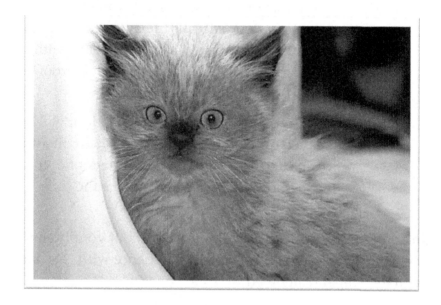

People who have not gone through the process of purchasing a pedigree cat may have some completely erroneous assumptions about what will happen when they visit a cattery.

If you think that you are simply going to drop in, pick a kitten, and pay for it, you need to sit down. It's not going to be that simple, and you may get turned down. Yes. You may get turned down.

If a breeder doesn't think you're a good candidate to raise one of their kittens, they don't have to do business with you — and they won't.

Understanding Breeder Requirements

Expect to be required to sign a written contract that will have some or all of the following stipulations:

- Sometime in the 72 hours following the adoption, you will take the kitten to a qualified veterinarian for a complete health evaluation. You will need to provide proof that this visit has occurred.

- Your agreement that the cat you adopt will be spayed or neutered before it reaches 6 months of age and that you will provide proof of this fact in order to gain possession of the cat's papers.

In addition, you will be asked questions about your home life, your schedule, and your prior experience with cats and with the Himalayan breed.

If you need to, adjust your attitude now! The breeder is not being a jerk or being nosy. They're doing their job — putting the welfare of the cats they raise first.

You may be asked things like, "Where do you plan for the kitten to sleep?" or "What do you intend to feed your cat?" Be honest with your answers. Don't try to "game" a breeder. It generally backfires.

If this is your first time to have a cat as a pet or to have this breed, say so. Ask questions. For instance, you might say something like, "My last cat loved to sleep on the bed. What do Himalayans usually prefer? I'll get the kitten whatever kind of bed he'd like best."

Breeders want to know that the kitten is going to a good home with loving and attentive "parents." Don't be at all surprised if the breeder calls you up during the first few weeks to check on the progress of the transition. You want this to happen!

Making friends with your breeder gives you access to someone who knows Himalayan cats well and can answer your questions. This is an important relationship, and one you want to cultivate.

Formulating Your Own Questions

Adopting a pedigree cat should be a process of give and take on both sides in the exchange of information. Any breeder that is not willing to answer your questions should be considered suspect.

In truth, talking to a breeder about their cattery usually opens the floodgates of information. Most are not only willing to talk about their cats, they're impossible to stop!

There are, however, some definite areas that you want to cover pre-adoption. Be sure that you go over these points to your satisfaction.

- Have the kitten's parents been healthy throughout their lives?

- Does the cattery maintain complete health records on all their cats and are you free to examine those records?

- Can you meet and interact with the kitten's parents?

- Has the kitten received any vaccinations and if so, when are the booster shots to be administered?

- Will you receive copies of all of the kitten's records at the time of adoption?

- Are there any specific health problems associated with Himalayan cats and has the kitten been evaluated for those issues?

- Has the kitten seen a vet for any other reason? If so, why and what treatment was administered?

- What is the nature of the health guarantee that is part of the adoption agreement?

- Has the kitten had fleas and has it required deworming?

- Ask for a complete summary of all veterinary care the kitten has received and copies of the complete records to pass on to your own veterinarian.

Understand that a kitten that has had or even does have fleas is not the end of the world. Catteries fight fleas on an ongoing basis. You just want to make sure that the "passengers" have disembarked from the baby before it comes into your home. Eradicating fleas can be a time consuming and exhausting process once they are established.

Also ask for the breeder's references. These should include people who have adopted kittens from the cattery in the past and who are willing to talk to you about the experience — both in terms of interaction with the breeder and their experience with the cat as a pet.

Ask About Socialization

In most cases catteries keep kittens until they are at least 3 months of age. This ensures that when the babies are adopted they have been fully weaned and they've become trained in the "basics," like litter box and scratching post use.

I'll discuss both of these things in greater detail later in the book, but you do want to specifically ask what kind of box and litter the kitten is accustomed to using and what kind of scratching surface.

The best way to reinforce and encourage good behavior in a newly adopted kitten is to keep everything exactly the same. For a smooth transition, use the same kind of box, litter, and post, only introducing changes gradually as the kitten grows.

Also find out how the breeder works with the kitten to make sure that it is well socialized.

Some of the hallmarks of a good program of socialization include:

- Daily handling
- Free exploration time
- Interaction with other cats and kittens
- Intellectual stimulation (toys and games)
- Supervised exposure to dogs and/or children
- Comfort level with reasonable noise

Kittens that have gotten used to these kinds of environmental factors early on tend to show much less nervousness as adult cats and more flexibility and adaptability to changes in their immediate surroundings.

Himalayans have a reputation for being intelligent, calm, and affable by nature, but the importance of socialization cannot be overstated. Cats are individuals and they will react to the manner in which they are raised.

If you've ever seen those funny cartoons that suggest pets and owners look alike, you may understand this point more fully. A nervous person tends to have nervous pets; a grumpy person's pets may be irascible, and so on.

Although Himalayan cats are generally even tempered, they do have Siamese blood and if truly pushed to their limits, they will react. That being said, however, any cat will display ill temper if something is going on that frightens, threatens, or simply displeases it.

Most breeders are in agreement, however, that a well socialized cat of any breed will be much more likely to exhibit the most positive qualities of its kind.

Judging the Health of a Kitten

You are not just visiting a cattery to inspect the facilities and to be evaluated by the breeder, you are also there to look at cats — which is actually the best part!

Always ask permission to handle the cats. Even though it's assumed that you are there to do so, it's just polite. If you're asked to use a hand sanitizer first, don't be offended.

Many feline diseases are so easily communicable they can be passed from one cat to another with just a nose tap. Sanitizing your hands is for the protection of the cats, and not a reflection on you.

When you are handling the kittens, pay attention to all the following factors:

- The kitten's coat should be soft, clean, and completely intact. There should be no evidence of thin spots or any missing patches of hair.

- Very gently blow on the fur to create a parting. Look at the skin. There should be no flaking, which would indicate that the skin is dry.

- Look behind the ears, in the "arm pits," and at the base of the tail. These are the prime locations for evidence of flea "dirt," small accumulations of what looks like tiny gravel, but is actually excreted blood from the fleas.

- Also look inside the ears. The flaps should be pink and healthy in appearance and the ear canal should be clean and free of black, tarry debris. There should be no odor, especially one that smells of yeast.

- Take a good look at the baby's eyes. You should be met with a bright, curious gaze that is both interested and sweet. The eyes should not be "runny" with discharge, and there should be no crusting in the corners.

- Also check the kitten's nostrils for any sign of discharge.

- The baby should not be sneezing or otherwise sniffling.

Don't be surprised if the kitten is a little shy when you're first introduced. That's normal. Within minutes, however, you should be interacting with a little ball of madcap energy!

Expect Paperwork

You are, after all, engaging in a transaction, so anticipate a fair amount of paperwork. The basic agreement will include the following:

- A description of the Himalayan breed.

- A description of the color and pattern of the specific individual being adopted.

- The gender of the kitten.

- The agreed upon price.

- The names of the parents.

- Contact information for both the buyer and the seller.

Specific provisions of the contract may include:

- A promise to provide ongoing and regular veterinary care including the recommended course of vaccinations.

- Agreement to meet the cat's specific grooming needs on a regular basis.

- A statement that no refund will be provided if that cat is returned for any reason.

Returns are a serious matter for breeders. The paperwork will include your agreement to a provision forbidding the giving away or selling of the cat without the breeder's permission.

Breeders are primarily concerned about the welfare of the cat. They do not want to see the animal wind up in any kind of shelter or pet store. Breeders would rather take kittens back than see that happen.

This is extremely important to emphasize. If at any point you feel that you can no longer keep the cat CONTACT THE BREEDER.

You will have to have the cat tested for ringworm, FELV/FIV, and fecal parasites before you return it, but you will always have a safe place to rehouse your cat if that proves to be necessary.

Required Spaying and Neutering

For the most part, people who work with breeders are acquiring kittens that have been judged to "pet quality." For whatever reason, the animal you are adopting is not considered a proper example of the breed for show or breeding purposes.

Don't let that concern you! You probably won't be able to recognize the flaw even if the breeder tells you what it is! You will, however, have to agree that before the baby reaches six months of age, it will be spayed or neutered.

Since this is the medically recommended period of time for either surgery to occur, this is a reasonable request by a cattery that has every right to protect its bloodlines.

The typical arrangement is that you do not receive the cat's papers until you have provided the cattery with a veterinary receipt showing that the spaying or neutering procedure has been performed.

Declawing Prohibited

Do not be surprised that the adoption agreement will expressly forbid declawing the cat in strongly worded terms. This surgery is illegal in Europe and in many parts of the United States for the simple reason that it is inhumane and completely unnecessary.

In order to remove the claw, the last digit of the cat's toe must be amputated. The procedure is painful, it affects the animal's mobility for the duration of its life, and it takes away the cat's primary means of self-defense.

Cats that have been introduced to scratching apparatus early in their life and whose claws are regularly clipped are not destructive.

Declawing is a radical measure done exclusively for the convenience of the owner and is a callous disregard of the welfare of the cat.

Known Health Conditions

In the chapter on health, I'll cover some of the medical issues associated with Himalayan cats, including those that are genetic in nature. Just remember that when you are adopting a pedigree Himalayan, the paperwork should include a health guarantee.

There should also be a statement about the parents' health, and an indication of what evaluations and tests they have received as well as a statement of the results.

Remember that the requirement for an initial health evaluation on your part, usually within 72 hours of the time you take possession of the kitten, provides a baseline for the health guarantee. This measure protects the cat *and* you.

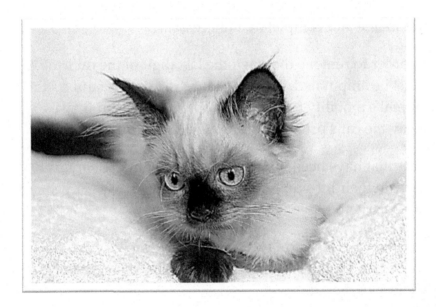

Preparing to Bring a Kitten Home

If you don't know it already, let me stress something that is pretty much a constant with all cats irrespective of breed — they do NOT like change. From a very early age, most cats get used to things being one way and they'd prefer that not change.

It is especially important when transitioning a kitten from a cattery to your home that everything stays the same, particularly regarding litter box arrangement and food.

Ask the breeder what kind of box the kitten has become accustomed to. You will want to know the style of the box, the height, and the kind of litter used.

Cats are very sensitive about litter texture. An abrupt change can put a cat off its box and lead to all kinds of problems. The same is true of litter box style.

I have had cats that absolutely would not use an open box under any circumstances, demanding the privacy of a covered tray.

Any changes to a cat's routine, especially in regard to the litter box, must be introduced slowly. Go in prepared to meet defeat. There may well be no more stubborn creature on the planet than a cat that has made up its mind about something.

Diet will be discussed at length in the daily care chapter, but you certainly do not want to subject a kitten to an abrupt food change. That is an open invitation for gastrointestinal upset.

Ask the breeder what the kitten has been eating and what dietary program they use with their maturing cats. Follow this advice to the letter, again, only introducing changes very slowly.

You will want to have some kitten safe toys on hand for the baby's homecoming. Don't bother with anything that has catnip. Cats show no reaction to the herb until they are 6-9 months old.

Instead, concentrate on items that do not present any kind of choking hazard. Many cat toys will always be "with supervision only" items. These include anything with strings, feathers, bells and similar attached decorations.

Get an appropriate brush for a kitten's delicate skin and start getting your baby accustomed to being brushed from the beginning of your relationship.

It's likely the breeder will already have started acclimatize the cat to daily grooming, so you will want to ask about this routine and if possible, replicate it by time of day and implements used.

Approximate Costs

A pet quality Himalayan kitten typically sells for about $1,000 / £650. After that, however, the breed is no more expensive to keep than any other popular domestic cat.

On average, it costs $130 / £84.50 to keep a cat per month, or $1,560 / £1014 per year. For a complete understanding of the monthly costs associated with keeping a cat, please refer to Chapter 3 on daily care.

In the absence of a chronic illness requiring ongoing veterinary care, the bulk of your monthly expenses will be for food and litter. Approximately 75% of the amount will go directly to feeding your pet.

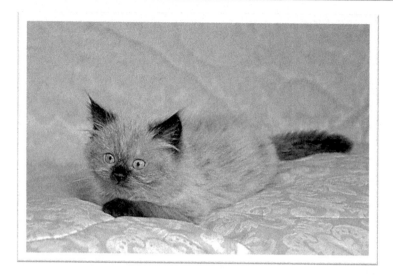

Never Rule Out a Rescue Cat Adoption

Obviously I'm a fan of the Himalayan breed or I wouldn't be writing this book. They are wonderful cats with excellent dispositions that are a pleasing blend of the sharp intelligence of the Siamese and the gentle playfulness of the Persian.

But in truth, every breed and every individual feline has unique qualities that will endear it to someone looking to give a cat a "forever home." This book — indeed any cat book — would be incomplete without praising the work of "no kill" shelters and rescue groups the world over.

If your heart is set on owning a Himalayan, you will undoubtedly have a wonderful relationship with your new pet for many years to come. But if you are simply thinking about adopting a cat, and perhaps are already a bit nervous about the cost of a pedigree pet, please don't rule out a rescue adoption.

Giving an abandoned kitten or adult cat a "forever home" is one of the greatest acts of kindness an animal lover can perform, one for which you will be rewarded daily with the love and loyalty of an animal that might very well have died otherwise.

Check your local shelter and speak with your veterinarian to find rescue groups in your area. I assure you, there will be many. Trap/neuter/release programs work hard every day to stem the raging epidemic of unwanted stray animals, but it is still an epic and tragic problem.

If you do move forward with your plans to adopt a pedigree Himalayan, please remember the efforts of rescue groups with your kind donations. These endeavors are always underfunded and understaffed. They need your help, but more importantly, the cats need your help!

Human Health Considerations

Before you buy you also need to consider any implications to your own health. For example, do you know if you have an allergy or sensitivity to cats? I would recommend taking advice from your Doctor to ensure that you understand the implications to your own health and if necessary, are allergy tested.

Chapter 3 – Daily Care for Your Cat

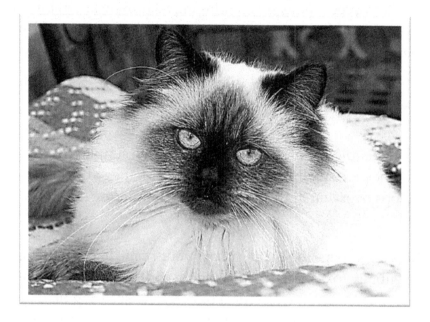

The basics of cat care are fairly standard for most breeds, with obvious differences for short and long-haired cats, or even for those, like the Sphinx, that have virtually no hair at all.

A great deal of successful feline husbandry involves understanding life from the perspective of your cat. In the case of the Himalayan, you are starting your relationship with your new pet with a distinct advantage.

One of the reasons this breed is so popular is that Himalayans tend to be playful and interactive without being destructive. They like to supervise and will be involved in whatever you're doing at the moment, but they are not insistent or annoying in their attentiveness.

This does not, however, negate the need to take some standard precautions when bringing a Himmie kitten into the household. All kittens think they're Bengal tigers and they can get into Bengal tiger-sized trouble fast!

The Need to "Kitten Proof"

Many people underestimate kittens for the simple reason that they are small — or at least you think they are until one gallops over you in the night or goes thundering down the hall.

Take basic steps to "kitten proof" your home like removing potentially toxic houseplants, taping cords and wires to the baseboards, capping electrical outlets, and securing or moving large heavy objects that could get pulled down or knocked over.

Fortunately, the breed is not destructive by nature. The problem with kittens — and this is true of any breed, not just Himalayans — is that they have zero judgment.

Kitten proofing the house, in this case, is much more about protecting your new little baby than taking care of your stuff. A good place to start is having a look at your houseplants and what you have growing outside.

Beware of Toxic Houseplants

Like many breeds, Himalayans are often tempted to start nibbling on houseplants. This bad habit is a double-edged sword. You may not enjoy the destruction of your plants, but you must also realize that many houseplants are actually quite toxic to cats.

The Cat Fancier's Association has produced a fairly comprehensive list of the most hazardous plants and it is always better to be overly cautious with vegetation and plant life. Of this lot, lilies are especially dangerous.

I appreciate it can be difficult to monitor and physically do anything about neighboring properties but any of the plants on this list should be kept strictly away from cats, and your pet should not be allowed into the garden if you have these items growing there or in your yard.

If your Himalayan eats any part of a plant you believe to be poisonous, seek the help of a qualified veterinarian immediately.

In Appendix 2, I have itemized this list as I think it is an important resource and I hope you will find it of assistance and reassurance in respect of the plants you may have growing in your garden or yard.

Making an Easy Transition

The best advice on helping your Himalayan kitten make a smooth transition to life with you will come directly from the breeder. These cats have many things going for them in terms of their adaptability and genial good humor.

Still, you will be bringing home a very young cat. No matter how big a kitten *thinks* he is, he's still a tiny little fellow and coming to live with you means he's leaving everything and everyone he knows. The more you can cushion this transition, the better.

At first, you will want to keep your new pet confined to a relatively contained area, or a completely segregated space if there are other cats in the house.

The best initial introductions with other pets are those conducted via the "sniff test" through a closed bedroom or bathroom door. This generally leads to a little exploratory under-the-door paw play as well.

Face-to-face introductions should always be supervised, but do not intervene unless it's absolutely necessary. Animals will pick up on our emotions. If you are nervous, they will be nervous.

Do not overreact, and if a "rescue" is necessary, just quickly and quietly pick up the kitten and return it to its own "room" until you're ready to try again.

Most cats need about a week to 10 days to become fully acclimatized to new surroundings. That's about the same length of time necessary for the hierarchy to get worked out in multiple pet households.

Don't be surprised if your kitten shoots to the top of that "pecking order." They can be veritable little tyrants, and those tiny claws are very, very sharp.

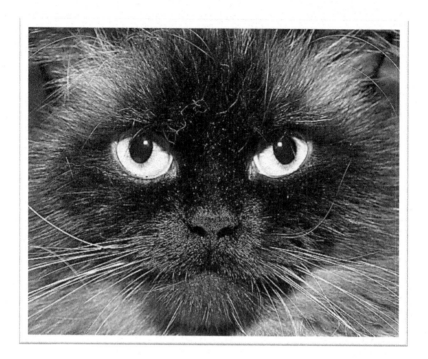

The Mind of a Cat

It's a commonly held belief that understanding the mind of a cat is next to impossible. The Himalayan, with those big, round Persian eyes can seem both guileless and impervious to being analyzed by a mere human all at the same time.

In truth, however, the majority of the stereotypes people entertain about cats are completely wrong. While some breeds are more reserved than others, that factor is more an individual trait than a genetic standard.

It is not uncommon for a cat to single out one person for special affection. While they may be friendly to others in the family, they will lavish their love, loyalty, and attention on their favorite.

Himalayans are good family pets and tend to be fairly egalitarian with their affections, but almost all cats will pick a favorite and bestow that person with extra attention. While I can't guarantee that will happen with your Himmie, don't be surprised if it does.

Additionally, cats are not the self-sufficient loners of the animal world people make them out to be. Some cats will do fine on their own during the day, but they will want your attention at night, even greeting you at the door to hear about your day. Himalayans fall into that category.

Purebred Siamese cats, on the other hand, are absolutely miserable when you're out of their sight. Thankfully this insistent neediness was bred out of the Himalayan.

When you bring a pet of any kind into your life, however, you're not just responsible for its care and feeding in a physical sense. You must also meet your pet's emotional needs.

Most behavior problems stem from an animal that is simply not getting enough attention. Cats get lonely, bored, and unhappy, and they let you know about it in the only ways that are available to them.

We tend to think of things like furniture shredding or knocking things over as a cat being "bad." In reality, those instances are examples of a cat trying to tell you something.

The one situation that absolutely makes me see red, and that I will write about at greater length later in this chapter, occurs when people turn their cats over to shelters due to poor litter box habits.

If you were to go into the home and look at the litter box, in 9 out of 10 cases, it will be filthy. Cats are fastidious creatures with a highly acute and well-developed sense of smell. They won't go in a urine-soaked box, and they have definite preferences in regard to litter texture and box design.

Even more serious, however, is the very real possibility that a cat that is going outside of the box has an undiagnosed kidney or bladder condition.

If a cat attempts to urinate in the box and experiences pain, it associates the discomfort with the location. The poor thing is just trying to find a place to go without hurting!

If you are a first-time cat owner, don't fall for such ridiculous and cruel stereotypes. The more you are engaged in your pet's day-to-day life, the better you will understand his language, and the better you can anticipate problems before they occur.

I have owned cats for more than 40 years and can attest to the unique qualities of each as an individual irrespective of breed. The important thing is that you spend time with your pet and learn how he communicates.

With every cat I've ever owned, I've been able to have complete wordless "conversations." That's part of the great joy of making your life with a cat, and the Himalayan is a perfect breed for this kind of bonding.

They are interestingly intuitive cats, observing their humans and picking up on subtle nuances of mood and behavior. As one of the more "supervisory" breeds, your Himalayan will soon learn your schedule and will be very appreciative if you don't deviate from the norm, thank you!

While they like routine, however, what a Himmie really wants is quality time each day with his human. This level of receptiveness to attention means that over the course of the cat's lifetime, you and your Himalayan will get to know each other very well. You will begin to communicate much more effectively than you may have thought possible.

I actually do not find cats inscrutable at all. They may deliver their messages differently than dogs, a much more effusive species, but cats still get their meaning across quite clearly if you know how to read their body language, facial expressions, and vocal intonations.

Dietary and Nutritional Information

Your emphasis in selecting foods for your cat should always be on quality. Based on the advice you initially receive from your breeder, and then from your veterinarian, buy the best food you can afford.

The following information and guidelines will help you to further refine the choices you make to optimize your cat's nutritional intake.

Wet or Dry?

This is the initial question most pet owners face. The tendency is all too often to go with dry due to the convenience both in serving the food, and in the belief that using dry food will make litter box maintenance easier.

This is a mistake. Cats are carnivores. Wet food provides them with a vital source of hydration, and cats that are fed canned food are less prone to gain weight than those that receive dry food only.

The best choice for your Himalayan is to feed a healthy mixture of wet and dry food that provides not only the correct mixture of nutrients, but also the tastes and textures your pet will enjoy.

A Note on Weight

Before we discuss actually choosing foods, let me give you a quick tip on how to judge the shape of your cat's figure.

If you stand over your cat and look down at his body while he is also standing, you should be able to see a slight indentation just behind the rib cage.

This is an excellent sign that your cat's weight is being maintained at a healthy level. If you can't see any "hips," Fluffy is probably getting a little too heavy.

Don't ever let your cats get started on human food. Many of the things we eat simply aren't good for our feline friends (more on that in just a minute), but giving a cat human food is an invitation to health problems.

Once a cat starts to become overweight, it's just a small step to conditions like diabetes, heart problems and joint diseases. Cats are skilled beggars. Use your will power! Don't fall down that slippery slope.

Dangerous "People" Foods

There are many things that we eat every day that a cat should never touch due to their toxicity in the feline system. These items include, but are not limited to:

- alcoholic beverages
- avocados
- grapes / raisins

- eggs

- garlic

- onions

- chives

- yeast dough

- caffeine in any form

- chocolate

The toxic elements present in chocolate are substances called methylxanthines, which are found in cacao seeds. A similar extract is used in soda beverages, which a cat should never be allowed to consume.

Cats that have been exposed to chocolate or to sodas can exhibit symptoms that are severe to the point of being life threatening. These may include:

- excessive thirst

- panting

- vomiting

- diarrhea

- irregular heartbeat

- seizures

- tremors

Sodas also contain sweeteners that include xylitol, which can cause liver failure in cats. Err on the safe side, and keep your pet away from all sweet items.

Salty foods are equally dangerous as they can cause rapid dehydration, creating a serious health risk.

Adult cats do not require milk and they actually don't get a lot of nutritional value from consuming it. All mammals produce milk that is correct for their own young, and, to state the obvious, cats aren't cows.

Cats and Milk

Although milk is not necessarily toxic to cats, it's also not the be all and end all of the feline diet as many people believe. A large percentage of cats are as lactose intolerant as their human keepers.

Felines do not produce sufficient amounts of the enzyme lactase. This means they do not efficiently digest cow's milk and are subject to gastrointestinal upset and diarrhea if they are given too much dairy content in their diets.

You can certainly offer your cat milk or cream occasionally as a treat, but if there is any sign of stomach upset or discomfort, discontinue the practice.

Reading Labels

When you read the label of a food you are considering for your pet, never lose sight of the fact that cats are meat eaters. If the first item on the label is not meat, look at another food.

As a general rule, the cheaper foods contain much more plant material as filler, while the more expensive or premium foods have a greater amount of meat.

There are so many kinds of cat food on the market it's best to go with breeder and veterinarian recommendations and your own budget in making a specific selection.

Estimating Food Costs

With the great variety of foods on the market, offering a clear estimate of food costs is all but impossible.

Conservatively, and based entirely on my own experience, you will likely spend $50 / £32.50 each month on wet food with $25 / £16.25 going for dry in the same period.

I don't recommend that dry food be left out for your Himalayan at all times. Try to limit the amount of dry food to a quarter to half a cup per day or 2 to 4 ounces / 56.7 to 113 grams.

Put out wet food once to twice per day. These servings should be roughly 5.5 ounces / 156 grams each.

Food and Water Bowls

For the most part you will be able to use plain bowls for both food and water, but you do need to be aware of a potential sensitivity called "whisker stress."

Some cats do not like the feeling of their whiskers dragging against the side of a bowl. You can tell that this is happening if your pet routinely picks up food and drops it on the floor to eat it.

Try switching to a receptacle that is more like a tray to cut down on the irritating sensation for your pet. There are products made specifically for cats for this purpose.

Normal food and water bowls will each cost $5 - $10 / £3.25 - £6.50. Try to use either stainless steel or crockery as plastic has a tendency to cause a breaking out on cat's chins that is commonly referred to as feline acne.

If you do opt for a bowl designed to reduce whisker stress, you will spend about $25 / £16.25. These trays typically come with legs or a stand to make them more stable and are thus slightly more expensive.

Be sure that your cat has a constant supply of clean drinking water. Some cats far prefer to drink running water, and I am a big fan of feline water fountains. These units sell for $30 / £19.50.

The Raw Diet Considered

Many pet owners over the past few years have been attracted to the idea of giving their pets, both dogs and cats the "raw" diet. The idea is to provide the animals with the kind of nutritional intake they would receive if they were hunting on their own.

Please understand that I mention this here not to advocate the diet or to instruct you in the proper administration of this dietary program. If you are interested in "feeding raw," you must research this topic thoroughly and discuss it with your veterinarian. Be prepared to hear serious reservations.

The majority of veterinarians and many cat experts do not believe that the raw concept is a good one since it includes bones. Even ground, bone shards can severely lacerate a cat's throat and intestines.

This, and the risk of salmonella poisoning, makes raw feeding for cats a questionable proposition. Certainly there is much more to this process than simply putting raw meat in your cat's bowl.

If you are interested in raw feeding, you have to learn how to do it, and you have to have the correct equipment. Strict standards of sanitation must be met, and only raw beef and chicken can be used.

All uneaten food, even if it has been refrigerated, must be discarded after 2-3 days and none of the food can ever be microwaved.

Just because your cat is a carnivore by nature, do not feel that a raw diet is necessary and do not proceed with such a feeding program without expert advice and adequate research.

Managing the Litter Box

In the beginning use the type of box to which the kitten has become accustomed at the breeder's. Also use the same kind of litter.

Any time you decide to try a different box or litter type, always leave the original arrangement in place until you know your cat will use the new option.

If your cat does go outside the box, you must clean the area with special enzymatic cleaners like those produced by Nature's Miracle ($5 - $10 / £3.25 - £6.50).

Cats interpret the world as a complex mix of smells. Any time your cat has urinated or defecated on a spot, and can still detect the scents he has left there, he may well consider that place acceptable to do his "business."

Picking a Litter

Whereas once the only commercially available litter was standard clay gravel, there are now many choices for cat owners to consider.

Clay Gravel

Clay gravel remains the tried and true traditional approach and it is also the cheapest. You can purchase 10 lbs. / 4.54 kg of this material for as little as $2.50 - $5.00 / £1.66 - £3.25.

The major drawback with clay gravel is the amount of dust it produces, and its low capacity to absorb moisture and control odor.

Clumping Sand

Clumping sand has become one of the most popular litters on the market. While it also generates dust, and has a capacity to fly all over the place if you have a cat who likes to dig, clumping litters have much better odor and moisture control.

Remember, if you are using a clumping litter, do not flush the clumps unless the mixture specifically says, "flushable." Regular clumping litter will absolutely destroy your plumbing, essentially turning to concrete in your pipes.

Clumping litter is more expensive than clay, but it is available in large amounts, for instance, you can purchase 42 lbs. / 19.51 kg. for $18 / £11.70.

Multiple cat mixes or those that claim extra odor controlling properties may be extremely pricey, however, with only 1.4 lbs. / 0.63 kg retailing for as much as $30 / £19.50.

"Green" Litters

Cat litters that are plant-based are generally made of materials like pine. They can be cost effective and are certainly environmentally friendly, but not all cats will use them.

Because the shavings are so lightweight, some cats don't seem to think they "feel" right. Never underestimate how sensitive cats are to texture, in many areas of their lives.

If your cat will use green litters, you will pay around $10 / £6.50 for 30 lbs. / 13.61 kg.

Absorbing Crystals

Crystals are the latest innovation in cat litters, and are touted for their ability to cut down on the potential for bacterial growth. The silica gel from which the crystals are made traps urine and holds it, allowing for a dry box and easier clean up.

Again, this is a matter of texture for the cat's paws. Not all cats will use crystals, and they are expensive, albeit effective. On average, 8 lbs. /3.63 kg of absorbing crystals sells for $16 / £10.40.

Picking a Box

After you have made your choice of litter type, you must consider what kind of box to offer your cat. Again, in the beginning, use what the kitten thinks is "normal" based on its experience at the cattery.

Your major options in this area start with the tried and true open pan. This is a cheap avenue at just $6 - $10 / £3.90 - £6.50, but there are drawbacks.

Open pans allow cats that like to scratch to fling litter far and wide, and they are a nightmare when it comes to dust control.

Many cats don't like open pans because they don't care to be watched. Additionally, open pans are unsightly. Homeowners have to find some place to both hide the pan and make it accessible to the cat, which can be a challenge.

Covered boxes answer many of these issues, giving the cat privacy, and hiding the mess. Since the lids are typically outfitted with a filter, a covered box will cut down on both dust and odor.

Depending on the size and shape of the box (square, rectangular, round, or triangular to fit in corners), you will spend $30 - $50 / £19.50 - £32.50 for a covered litter box.

The latest innovation is the self-scooping box, which humans love and cats treat with fascination, suspicion or open horror.

Self-scooping boxes require electricity since they employ a scoop activated by a motion sensor that is tripped when the cat exits the pan. The scoop rakes through the litter, depositing the soiled material in a closed receptacle.

When the receptacle is full, simply cap it with a provided lid and throw it away, putting a fresh disposable refill in its place.

If your cat does not react with fear to the mechanism, this can be an excellent solution for cat owners who are weary of scooping. This kind of automated arrangement costs approximately $150 - $200 / £97.50 - £130.

Be warned. If you decide to try a self-scooping box, keep your old pan in place. Fluffy may well rebel at this idea and demand his old "out house" back.

The Himalayan at Play

The Himalayan is a very playful breed. They especially like games of "fetch," and most will cheerfully run after a crumpled wad of paper over and over again. They also like small toys they can toss and bat about. Their play is much more vigorous than that of a Persian, but not at all destructive.

Unlike their Siamese cousins, Himmies are not vigorous scratchers, so a simple carpeted scratching pole retailing for $30 / £19.50 will do nicely for this breed. However, since they also have all that regal Persian blood, they won't mind in the slightest if you spend $100 - $300 / £65 - £195 for an elaborate cat tree outfitted with platforms, tunnels, perches, and ramps.

If your Himmie does show an unhealthy interest in your furniture, you can discourage this behavior with pennyroyal or orange essence sprays at $12 - $15 / £7.80 - £9.75 or double-side adhesive strips at $8 - $10 / £5.20 - £6.50.

Speaking Cat

Cats have a complex language that is built not just on vocalizations, but also on facial expression and body language. Most people think, for instance, that when a cat rubs up against his human, it's an expression of affection. Try "ownership."

When your cat is rubbing up against you, he's using the scent glands located around his mouth to mark you as his territory. Now, granted, you may have "most favored nation" status, but the rubbing has pretty much the same purpose whether it's you or the edge of the coffee table.

When a cat leans into you with his whole weight or "bonks" you with his head, this is more of an expression of camaraderie and affection - and likely a request for an ear scratching or a chin rub. This is the same message a cat is sending when he insinuates himself between you and the laptop screen or plops down on your book.

Some other bits of body language that are clear messages if you know how to read them include:

- Picking up a paw and shaking it with an expression of disgust -- because that's exactly what the cat is saying. "I don't like how this feels, smells, or tastes. Yuck!"

- Lashing the tail about. Surely you know this one! A cat with a lashing tail is not happy, to the point of being actively peeved. Especially if your pet's ears are back and his eyes are narrowed; let him have some time to calm down.

- Holding the tail straight up. This is the best expression of a feline good mood you can see. That tail might as well be a flag emblazoned with the word, "Happy!"

- Holding the tail straight out from the body. Think of this one as lowering the flag a bit. Now the message is, "Hmm. I'm not sure about this." Your cat isn't yet in a bad mood, but he's definitely checking the temperature of things.

- Holding the tail down. Now the flag has been run down the pole. Your cat is not happy, and he's likely exiting the room. A tail held down can indicate fear, or unease with the situation.

A cat that has just broken a flower pot won't apologize, but he's smart enough to know you're not going to be thrilled with him, so being elsewhere is, in his mind, a great idea.

While many of these cues are universal to all cats, remember that every cat is an individual. The real way to "get" your cat's message is just cultivating familiarity over long association. Most cat owners don't need interpreters to know what their cat is saying or to figure out the opinion their pet is expressing.

All dyed in the wool cat people know, "the look," which is usually delivered with withering proficiency right after you've put something sub-standard in kitty's bowl. "The look" is a commentary on human intelligence, and we don't rate well in that moment!

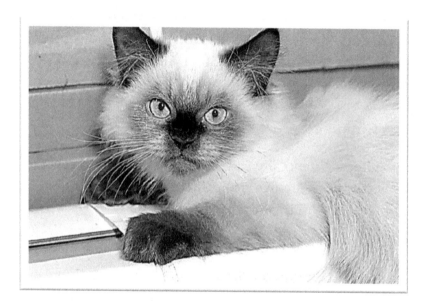

Grooming Requirements

Tangles and mats are one of the biggest concerns in maintaining a longhaired cat's coat. On a daily basis you should use a shedding comb to remove loose hair from your Himmie's fur to prevent these issues.

Matted hair is not only unsightly, but also unhealthy, blocking air flow to the skin and creating an environment ripe for skin irritation and itching.

Shedding combs have a combination of long and short wire teeth in alternating rows. They retail for $10 / £6.50 or less.

If mats do develop, it is not advisable for you to attempt to cut them out on your own. Cats have fragile skin that is easily damaged.

For minor mats, you can try to work them out starting at the base and gently teasing the hairs apart. If, however, you cannot successfully loosen the mat, take your pet to a professional groomer.

Claw Clipping

Claw clipping generally can be done safely at home, and is always the first step in a professional grooming session. To complete this chore safely:

- Place your Himmie on your lap.

- Pick up one front paw.

- Apply gentle pressure with your thumb behind the toes.

- With the claws extended, examine the nail.

- The claw is translucent.

- The vascular "quick" is pink.

- Snip off only the clear tips.

- Do not forget the dewclaw on the side of the foot.

Be extremely careful not to nip the "quick" as this will not only cause your pet pain, but result in profuse bleeding.

Try not to hold your cat down. "Less restraint" is better because no cat likes to feel trapped. With practice, you can safely and quickly trim your pet's nails before the cat even realizes what is happening but I've found Himalayans to be fairly compliant with claw clipping.

Buy clippers specifically designed for pets. Those with plier grips are easy to use and offer superior control. They are priced at approximately $10 / £6.50.

If you are in any way nervous about doing this, it would be a wise precaution to ask your vet to show you how to trim your cats nails on the first occasion.

Testing Your Cat's Tolerance

For many people the idea of giving a cat a bath sounds like a recipe for disaster. Frankly, it can be, but generally Himalayans are good about this process, especially if they've been introduced to bathing from an early age.

If, however, you have adopted an older animal, you may want to try the "tail test." If you put your cat's tail in the water and the animal goes ballistic, then you know that a professional groomer is going to have to take over.

The same method will work with the blow dryer. Turn the unit on once and you'll know in about 2 seconds how your Himmie is going to feel about the "monster."

The Actual Bath

If your Himmie is agreeable and you go ahead with the bath, assemble all of your supplies and have them close by. The last thing you want to do is turn loose a wet cat! Keep the bath water lukewarm, but no hotter.

Himalayans have thick coats, so you will need to make sure the water penetrates all the way to the base. Don't let water get in your pet's ears, eyes, or nose. Although not all cats will stand for it, soft cotton balls tucked just inside the ear are a good precaution.

Do not ever pour water over the cat's face. Instead, clean this area with a warm washcloth. Do not use soap around your pet's eyes.

Degreasing the Coat

When you Himmie is completely wet, start with a degreasing formula that is formulated for use with dogs and cats. Degreasers come in both paste and gel forms and are used exactly like shampoo. Expect to pay approximately $15 / £9.75 for 16 ounces / 454 grams.

Always rinse degreaser out of your pet's fur completely. You will know the cat's hair is clean when it feels velvety to the touch even though the animal is wet.

Using Shampoo

Always use a hypoallergenic, natural shampoo on your cat. These products sell in a price range of $10 - $15 / £6.50 - £9.75 for 16 ounces / 454 grams.

Be very gentle when applying the shampoo. Don't scrub, as this action will cause tangling. Rinse repeatedly so as to leave no residue in the coat.

When the shampoo is out of the coat, drain the sink or tub. Run your hands through the cat's fur in a straight, downward motion to get as much excess water out of the fur as possible.

Wrap your pet in a soft, dry towel and use the same kind of even strokes to continue drying the hair. Again, avoid any "scrubbing" action.

If your cat will allow it, finish the grooming session by blow drying the animal's fur at the lowest possible setting while gently combing or brushing the hair with straight, even motions.

Clipping and Trimming Fur

It is not a good idea to trim or clip your Himmie's fur at home. The risk of seriously hurting your pet is too great. Due to the density of a Himalayan's fur, it is common for the belly and inside of the legs to require trimming.

Note, however, that this kind of cut should not be performed on animals that are going to be exhibited in a cat show. Trimming the "undercarriage" is only appropriate for household pets.

In warmer regions, many longhaired cats receive a "lion cut." The body is shaved, with a "mane" at the neck and "cuffs" at the ankles left in place. This gives your cat relief from the heat, and you a break from much of the daily brushing.

Attending to Eye Care

Since Himalayans do have Persian blood, they can be plagued with tearing eyes and facial staining. In order to clean your cat's face, use a foam cosmetic disc dipped in warm water.

Gently wipe at the corner of the cat's eyes with a soft, downward motion. You can use the same method for any nasal drainage present.

Caring for the Ears

Ear care really should be left to a professional groomer or to your veterinarian. If you see black, tarry debris on the ear or just inside the ear, you can softly clean the area with a cotton ball dipped in warm water. Do not ever insert a cotton swab in the ear canal.

Excessive thick, tarry debris and a yeasty smell indicates the presence of ear mites, necessitating a visit to the veterinarian.

Evaluating Professional Groomers

While Himalayans will benefit from monthly grooming, some owners find they can take their pets to a professional groomer every 2-3 months with no serious problems resulting.

Under the best circumstances, you will be able to find a groomer who will come to your home to work with your Himmie. Very few cats of any breed like to be taken out of their familiar environment. Cats are always calmer when everything around them is "theirs."

Ask your breeder for references for local groomers, and inquire at your vet clinic. Most practices keep a bulletin board in the waiting room where groomers and pet sitters leave their flyers or business cards.

Always visit a grooming facility or interview a groomer before booking an appointment for your pet. You want to see how the animals are secured against escape and ensure that the place is clean and well maintained.

Specifically ensure that the establishment requires all client animals to be current with their vaccinations. Feline diseases are highly contagious, so the cats should be kept strictly separated while on the premises.

Grooming costs can vary rather widely, but typically a single session will cost approximately $50 / £32.50.

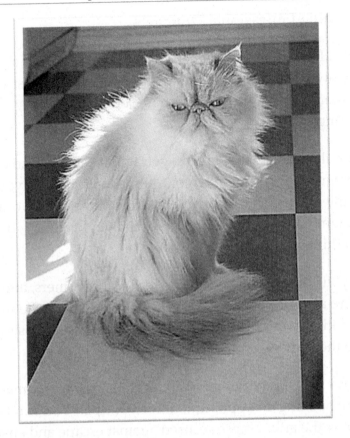

Time Away from Your Cat

All pet owners face one common concern: What happens when it is time to go on vacation? Many people travel with their pets, but the fact is pets cannot always go with their families. What will you do with your cat when you have to go away from home – on vacation or out of town for business or for a funeral, for example?

Consider who will look after your cat before the need ever arises. You have several options. Perhaps a friend or a family member, who has been around your cat and feels comfortable, can call to your home to care for it.

Pet sitters are also a popular option, especially in the United States where pet sitting businesses must be licensed and insured to operate. A pet sitter generally comes to your home to visit your pet – to ensure he has food, water, and time out to exercise. Pet sitters typically charge per visit, and you can schedule several visits each day.

Is a pet sitter a viable option for your cat? That depends. How long will you be gone? Can you afford to have the pet sitter come each day to ensure your cat is looked after as you wish? Be sure, if you look for a pet sitter, to find someone who has experience caring for cats. Before you hire a pet sitter or agree to a visiting schedule, the pet sitter will generally come to your home for an initial consultation. During that meeting, you will talk with the pet sitter about your cat, its schedule, diet, and any other concern you may have. But, more importantly, the meeting will allow your cat and the pet sitter to meet and to become comfortable around each other. Some pet sitters charge for this initial meeting, but many do not.

You can find pet sitters in the United States through the National Association of Pet Sitters (www.petsitters.org) and Pet Sitters International (http://www.petsit.com). A comprehensive list of pet sitters in the United Kingdom can be found through the National Association of Registered Pet Sitters (www.dogsit.com) and yes, they look after more than dogs and don't have any trouble with cats!

Make sure that your pet sitter is insured and fully referenced as they will have access to you home and your pet. You should also contact your home insurance providers to confirm your cover is not affected by having a pet sitter stay at your home.

If you do not like the idea of a pet sitter, then some rescue organizations offer boarding and pet sitting services while others may just be able to provide you with recommendations of sitters.

If you have trouble finding someone you trust or don't want to become a burden to family and friends then you may want to consider boarding.

Boarding Your Himalayan

If it should prove necessary to board your Himalayan while you are away or due to other life circumstances, you'll find that your pet will tend to react to the experience with his usual calm demeanor.

In all likelihood, you will be much more nervous than your cat about the whole boarding process! If your regular veterinarian does not offer boarding services, here are some guidelines to help you choose a boarding facility:

- Begin checking out facilities well in advance of your trip, especially if it coincides with a major holiday. These places fill up quickly.

- If possible, find a boarder that caters to cats only or that keep their feline clients well segregated from dogs and other pets. Cats like quiet, especially when they are in an unfamiliar place.

- Make sure that your pet's food and water intake is closely monitored, especially in the first 24-48 hours. Cats can become dehydrated quickly when they are stressed, which can lead to serious health problems.

- If there is a health problem, does the facility have a vet on staff and what provisions can be made for that person to immediately contact your cat's regular vet?

- Will your cat require any vaccinations or boosters before being allowed to board at the establishment? Do you need to supply any medical records prior to the stay?

- Make sure that your cat will be housed in a spacious enclosure alone. Cats, unlike dogs, do not want to mingle. Additionally, many feline diseases are highly transmittable by nothing more than a nose tap.

- If you have more than one cat and will be boarding both, make sure they will be allowed to remain together in the same enclosure.

Be sure to schedule a time to tour the facility. Ask for references, and discuss the facility you are considering with your veterinarian.

Always transport your cat in a secure cat carrier. Never allow your pet to ride in the car unless it is inside its crate, which should be securely locked.

Coming Home Again

How will your cat react when you return home, especially if you have been gone a considerable period? Well, cats are like people, so do not be surprised if your beloved friend is angry with you for having left them. And, like people, he will need time to shed that anger. On the other hand, cats while being extremely independent may just give you a look that says "Oh it's you!" and then won't leave your side for days in case you disappear again.

Chapter 4 – Senior Moments

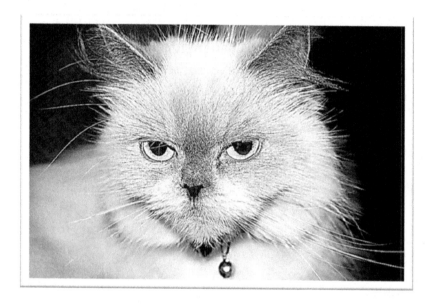

Not all cats age the same way, any more than all humans experience the same age-related problems. I have had cats with arthritis, one that went blind, and others that developed benign fatty tumors called lipomas.

The signs of aging tend to be gradual. Some of the most typical are included in this chapter.

Less Acute Senses

You may begin to notice subtle signs that your cat is not hearing or seeing as well as it once did. These changes may, however, completely escape your attention.

Some years ago one of my senior cats who went blind compensated so well that I had no idea anything was wrong until I rearranged the living room furniture.

Her obvious confusion led me to schedule a vet visit and we discovered that not only was she blind, but that she was suffering from high blood pressure and needed medication.

Obviously no cat that has vision or hearing loss should ever be allowed outdoors. I am not a fan of "outside" cats anyway, as our modern world is far too dangerous for our beloved pets.

Frankly, I would be more concerned about your cat's senses of smell and taste. Deficits with these two abilities can adversely affect your pet's appetite and lead to weight loss. Cats won't eat what they can't smell, so it may be necessary to alter an older cat's diet.

Consult with your vet first so that you don't give a senior cat something that will cause gastrointestinal upset. If your cat isn't used to eating "fishy" foods, they may like the smell, but get an upset tummy from the richer fare.

You can try just slightly warming your pet's existing wet food to increase the smell, but be very careful not to get it too hot. If you warm the food in the microwave, stir it well with a fork and let it cool to just slightly more than room temperature before you give it to your cat. Please ensure that any uneaten food is thrown away quickly to avoid the risk of bacterial growth and the food spoiling.

Changes in Appearance

It's perfectly normal for cats to lose muscle mass as they age, but always have any dramatic changes in weight, both losses and gains evaluated by your veterinarian.

Also pay close attention to the condition of an aging cat's coat. If your pet is not able to groom as well as he once did, you may need to step in and help with more frequent brushing.

Since the Himalayan's coat is thick and lush, be especially mindful about any thinning or matting. Both are signs of potential bad health.

Cats can develop arthritis the same way humans do and your pet may simply not be able to reach the hard spots any more. This may extend to "personal" areas.

Without annoying your cat, just make sure all is well under the tail. If cleaning there is necessary, gently use a warm washcloth and plain, clean water. Please ensure that you observe good hand hygiene and wash the cloth between uses.

Make sure the litter box is low enough for your pet to get in and out of easily. Since cats don't like changes in box type or litter consistency, consider trimming down the front edge of the box so your pet can step in and out more easily.

Changes in Mood and Behavior

The most important thing to do with a senior citizen cat is to be aware of subtle changes in mood and behavior. An older cat may no longer be able to jump up to the window sill, but would still like to sun. Give him a way to "stair step" to his favorite perch without jumping.

Himalayans are fairly mellow anyway, and become more so as senior citizens. All older cats tend to spend more time sleeping, and it can be quite difficult to distinguish this type of normal slowing down from actual illness.

Always remember that cats instinctively hide their pain and illness. Use your judgment and your understanding of your pet's nature. Never hesitate to schedule a vet visit. I always give the same advice, "If you think something is wrong with your cat, it probably is."

The last thing you need to worry about is being labeled a "crazy cat lady" or a "doting Dad." You know your pet better than anyone. Go with your gut, especially when it comes to older cats. Make the vet appointment if you think your cat is sick or just not doing well.

Regular Checkups

Make sure your older cat has regular checkups. Seniors are more likely to develop dental issues, and all skin growths should be evaluated.

Monitor changes in litter box habits that might signal a urinary tract infection or more serious kidney problems. If the cat is vomiting more than usual, a vet visit may be in order.

Drinking large amounts of water might indicate the presence of diabetes. Aging cats can also suffer from hyperthyroidism and high blood pressure, both of which are very treatable.

Because older cats sleep more, they are more prone to be cold. Make sure your senior has a warm bed and lots of quiet time. The warmth will also help if your pet is suffering from arthritis.

Treat your aging cats like what they are, little ladies and old gents with fur. Love them all the same, and make whatever changes you need to in their environment to keep them happy, engaged, and comfortable in their golden years.

Making the Hard Decision

Saying good-bye to a beloved companion of many years is both heartbreaking and a great act of love. Euthanasia is a difficult topic, both for you to read about and for me to write about.

I can only share with you what I believe to be the truth based on my personal experience. No one can tell you when it is time to make the hard decision but your cat.

Do not listen to anyone who makes you feel pressured to come to a decision. I promise you that you would resent this in the future if you do so.

Get the best medical information that you can from your veterinarian, conduct your own research, and simply be with your cat. I cared for a well-loved pet through a 25-month struggle with cancer.

The people in my life knew better than to try to offer advice. My veterinarian was kind, professional and honest. I will admit I spent money on treatments and medications I could not afford for the simple reason that my pet was enjoying his life and was still very much himself.

The day that he was not, he told me so. Only an "animal person" may understand what I mean, but I assure you my cat told me it was time to go. When he did, I called the vet and we gently and lovingly, helped him through that transition.

I have observed euthanasia from the perspective of a breaking heart. I can tell you with great certainty that when performed by caring, understanding veterinary professionals this is the ultimate act of compassion. My vet had a relationship both with my pet and with me.

She remains my good friend and I will always be grateful to her for the care she gave my feline companion to the very last moment of his life.

I cannot stress enough how important it is for you as a pet owner to have a vet with whom you can work in this way. I know this experience would have been truly horrible had I been dealing with a vet who did not understand both my cat's illness and my own emotional pain.

In the aftermath, allow yourself to grieve. You may have to find other "animal people" who will truly understand the loss you are suffering, but be assured that it is a valid loss of a living creature that has been part of your life and a member of your family.

The kindest thing anyone said to me as I struggled to keep my composure in the days following my pet's death was simply, "I am so sorry you lost your friend."

Our pets give us unconditional love, even when we are not being our best selves. The absence of that constancy is a deep loss and one that neither you nor anyone in your life should attempt to minimize.

Adopting a Senior Cat

People who adopt grown cats in need, especially seniors are, in my estimation very special angels. Many lovely older pets are put down every year when all they need is a loving second home.

You will be taking in an animal with established habits and preferences, and likely pre-existing needs, but there is no reason to think you cannot have a loving relationship with an older animal in its golden years.

If you are prepared to meet the special needs of a senior cat, including late in life veterinary expenses, giving an older, homeless cat a home is a vital part of feline rescue work. This is an area of that mission that always needs more willing volunteers.

Chapter 5 – Himalayan Cat Health

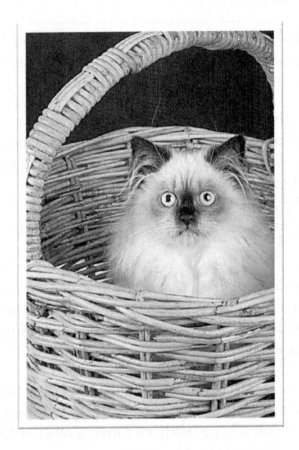

Ongoing preventive health care is the greatest medical service you can provide for your Himalayan. Think of yourself as your cat's primary health "insurance." The longer you live with your cat, the more you will know what is "normal" for your Himalayan.

One of the best pieces of advice cat owners can take to heart is this: if you think something is wrong with your pet, something is probably wrong. Never hesitate to take a companion animal to the vet for fear of being perceived as an over-protective "parent."

Cats hide sickness and pain for as long as they possibly can. This behavior is part of their survival instinct. As small carnivores, they have an innate awareness of their place in the food chain.

In the wild, the appearance of weakness increases the chance of potential predation from larger animals. Even the safest house cat cannot overcome the power of that instinct.

Finding a Vet

Sometimes the best way to find a great local vet is to ask others who own cats. If you do not know someone in your neighborhood with a cat, contact your local animal rescue or go online and find an online discussion group in your area and start asking for recommendations.

In addition to helping you find a good, qualified vet, other cat owners can help you avoid the not-so-desirable vets. Ask plenty of questions as to why the person recommends the particular vet. Is the vet personable and knowledgeable about cats in general? Does he or she have experience? Are their prices reasonable, in the person's opinion? Find out as much as you can as to why the person likes the vet. Also ask them what they do not like about the vet.

The Basics of Preventive Health Care

While interacting with your cat on a daily basis, be aware of the following signs of potential illness and follow up with a vet should any of these symptoms or behavioral changes appear in your Himalayan.

Changes in weight.

This can mean either a gain or a loss. Cats with a healthy weight have a pad of fat over the ribs, but the bones can still be felt through this layer. Looking down at the cat, you should be able to see an indentation behind the rib cage where the "hips" start.

Physical changes in gait including a reluctance to perform certain motions like running or jumping.

Essentially when a cat displays these kinds of "favoring" behaviors, there is a strong chance the animal is experiencing joint or muscle pain or that a growth is inhibiting normal movement.

Differences in the level of moisture on the nose.

This can extend to either a dry nose or an actual runny nose indicating the presence of a cold or an infection. A cat's nose under normal circumstances should be clean and dry, but not cracked. There should be no discharge from the nostrils, either clear or discolored.

Presence of discharge from the eyes.

While all cats occasionally get an accumulation of "matter" in the eyes, Himalayans, like Persians are prone to becoming tearful. If this is excessive with severe staining, it could indicate a physical abnormality that requires veterinary attention.

Always make sure the pupils of the eyes are equal and centered and that the whites are not discolored and have only minimal visible blood vessels.

Ear sensitivity and visible debris.

All cats have a tendency to develop ear infections and to occasionally have problems with ear mites and similar irritating parasites. A foul odor emanating from the ear is always a key warning sign.

The inner surface of the ear should be clean and smooth in appearance with no visible redness. If the area is inflamed, hot to the touch, and/or black debris is present, the cat's ears should be examined by the vet.

Pale gums and yellow discoloration on the teeth.

A cat's gums should be pink, and the teeth should be clean and white. Any dark or yellow build-up on the teeth is an indication that plaque is present.

Regular dental exams are also critical in detecting any lesions that might indicate the presence of an oral cancer. If found early, such growths can be managed with some success.

Dental care is an extremely important aspect of feline husbandry, with many cat owners actually brushing their cat's teeth using feline toothpaste and brushes available at the veterinary clinic. Never use human products for this purpose on a cat.

While such a regime may sound absolutely impossible, if started early in a cat's life, the animals are often quite amiable about the whole business. Since it's much more a matter of just getting the paste in the cat's mouth, some owners use their index finger as a "brush."

A dental care kit from a vet typically costs about $7 - $10 / £4.55 - £6.50. It's never too late to start looking after your cat's teeth, and it's certainly worth a try to see how your cat will respond to the process.

Don't worry. You won't lose a finger. If your cat doesn't want any part of dental care, he'll let you know fast enough!

What else to look out for.

There are other factors to consider in monitoring your cat's health on a daily basis.

- Have any growths, masses or bumps evaluated.
- Watch your cat's respiration. It should be from the chest, not the abdomen.
- If the cat goes outside the litter box, immediately have your pet evaluated for kidney and/or bladder infections.

Routine Elements of Health Care

No element of routine health care for your cat is more important than forging a positive relationship with a qualified veterinarian.

While it is true that any "small animal" vet can treat your Himalayan, I am an advocate of feline-specific practices when they are available.

Offices that are "cats only" tend to be much quieter and have fewer disturbing and threatening scents, which is soothing for patients with a nervous disposition. Himalayans are not typically skittish cats, but no pet likes to go to the doctor — any more than we do!

Any time you are considering using a veterinarian, it's a good idea to make an appointment just to interview the doctor. Explain why you are coming in and that you are perfectly willing to pay the usual fee.

Prepare any questions you have in advance. Be on time. Get the information you need, ask for a brief tour of the clinic, and do not overstay your welcome. Vets are busy medical professionals.

You want to get a sense of the vet's personality and the demeanor of the staff as well as the environment and condition of the clinic itself. Only if you are satisfied with what you see and hear should you make a second appointment to take your cat in.

Even at this point in time, however, don't consider the relationship a "done deal." Observe how the vet and the staff interact with your cat, and how your pet reacts to them.

This is not just a matter of you getting along with the vet, but of your cat being as comfortable as possible under the circumstances.

Spaying and Neutering

When you adopt a pet quality Himalayan from a breeder you will be required to agree to have your pet spayed or neutered before six months of age.

If you do not already have a veterinarian, this will be your first opportunity to get your pet established with a health care professional, so you will want to make careful decision in regard to these procedures.

Prices for spaying and neutering vary by clinic, and there are low cost options available for as little as $50 / £32.50, but this may not be the time to think about economy. Take the time to find a vet with whom you plan to work over the course of your cat's life.

It is a tremendous benefit to your cat's long-term wellbeing for all of its records to be in one place, and for one health care professional to have followed the cat's development through life. If you need a recommendation for a qualified vet, ask your breeder.

Vaccinations

Vaccinations have long been considered a standard aspect of preventive care for small companion animals, but the practice of administering these injections has not been without controversy in recent years. The primary concern is for the potential of tumors developing at the site of the injection.

If you have concerns about the wisdom of vaccinating your Himalayan you should discuss this matter with both the breeder and your veterinarian.

By the time you take possession of the kitten, it will undoubtedly have received the first round of shots, so you will have to decide if you wish to finish the course of injections or not.

The recommended course of inoculations includes the following vaccines:

Distemper Combo

This injection is administered at six weeks of age with recommended boosters every 3-4 weeks until the cat is 16 weeks old. A second booster will then be given at one year, with subsequent shots every three years for the remainder of your pet's life.

The standard injection is formulated to provide protection for panleukopenia (FPV or feline infectious enteritis), rhinotracheitis (FVR, an upper respiratory / pulmonary infection), and calicivirus (which causes respiratory infections).

There are variations of the vaccine that also provide protection against Chlamydophilia, which causes conjunctivitis.

Feline Leukemia

At 2 months of age the injection for feline leukemia is administered, with a booster to be given 3-4 weeks later. At one year of age, boosters are then given annually for life.

Feline leukemia is an extremely infectious disease that requires only a nose tap for transmission to occur between animals. If your pet is at any risk of coming into contact with cats that live outdoors, this vaccination is extremely important.

Rabies

Often owners do not have a choice about the administration of the rabies vaccine as it is mandated by local law. Proof of compliance is often required as well. Rabies vaccinations are priced at approximately $40 / £26.

Genetic Conditions

The following genetic conditions can be present in Persians in general and Himalayans specifically and should be among the topics you discuss with your breeder while negotiating an adoption.

Hypertrophic Cardiomyopathy

Hypertrophic cardiomyopathy (HCM) thickens the heart muscle causing fluid to accumulate in the lungs and blood clots to form. It can only be confirmed with an echocardiogram.

There is no cure for this condition, which ultimately causes the cat to die of heart failure. Do not believe any breeder that makes the claim that their line is totally free of HCM.

There is no way to guarantee that this genetic fault is not passed on, since, in truth, it can affect a cat of any breed. Most breeders are willing to discuss HCM openly, and to admit if it has been an issue among their cats.

Polycystic Kidney Disease (PKD)

Polycystic Kidney Disease (PKD) presents at birth with cysts in the kidneys. As the cat ages, the masses grow until they cause the kidneys to fail. PKD becomes detectable in the first 10 years of life; sometimes by the time the animal is 3 years old.

Potential symptoms can include poor appetite and weight loss, extreme thirst and excessive urination, and deterioration of the coat. The cat's gums will be pale from dehydration and it will have bad breath and often ulcers in the mouth. X-rays will show enlargement of the kidneys.

With special diets, the regular administration of subcutaneous fluids, hormone therapy, and antacids, PKD can be managed, but it cannot be cured. The prognosis varies by individual from months to years.

Idiopathic Facial Dermatitis

Idiopathic facial dermatitis typically becomes evident at about 2 years of age. It is a chronic skin disease that causes lesions that become progressively severe. There will be a black discharge around the eyes and nose. The ears become red and inflamed, and often there is significant trauma caused by the cat scratching itself.

The condition resists most long-term solutions, so treatment involves finding a management strategy that will work. The first line of treatment is usually corticosteroids, then cyclosporine. Medication will be required for life.

Entropion

With entropion, the cat's eyelids curl inward damaging the cornea, potentially blocking the tear ducts, and definitely causing irritation. The condition may affect either the upper or lower eyelids, and may be present in one or both eyes.

The cause may be trauma, or a congenital malformation like excessive skin folds. The first signs are usually excessive tearing, squinting, and redness in the eyes.

Generally excessive tearing does not require treatment, but if corneal ulcers develop, surgery to remove the excess skin folds is indicated. Entropion responds very well to treatment with an excellent long-term prognosis.

Blocked Tear Ducts

When excessive tearing is present, the cat's tear ducts may be blocked due to inflammation or scarring. Generally the only management strategy is to keep the area clean and dry.

If the ducts have to be flushed out to clear away the blockage, the cat must be heavily sedated. This should only be done after careful consideration and consultation, usually with a veterinarian who specializes in conditions of the eye.

Blocked tear ducts typically resist treatment and are often incurable, but they generally do not cause the cat any discomfort. The condition does, however, respond well to diligent maintenance on the part of the owner.

Dental Disorders

Persians and cats with Persian blood like the Himalayan often develop dental problems in relation to the shortness of their jaws and the potential flatness of their faces. Kittens can be born with poorly positioned or crowded teeth, which additionally create a climate ripe for periodontal disease.

These issues can cause the teeth to jut into the lips or gums with resulting abnormal wear, difficulty chewing, and trauma. Symptoms of such problems include bad breath, bleeding, chewing on one side, cocking the head while eating, and an inability to keep food in the mouth.

Such malformations generally become apparent at 14-24 weeks of age as the permanent teeth begin to come in. Cats with genetic mouth issues will need professional dental cleaning regularly. They often must be fed special diets and have oral rinses administered. It is not unusual for a dental surgeon to shorten or remove some of the affected teeth.

Once the malformation is detected and treated, the prognosis is typically good.

Wry Mouth or Wry Bite

An asymmetrical deviation of the lower jaw is called wry mouth or wry bite. The misplacement causes the cat's teeth to strike the lips or palate and often the animal cannot close its mouth.

Wry mouth is treated by removing or repositioning the teeth so the cat will have a comfortable bite and can chew properly.

Administering Medications

If you have already had cats in your life, you may have started chuckling just reading the header "administering medications."

Like any sub-culture, "cat people" have their own language. If told by another cat person, "I had to give my cat medicine," the response will likely be the rueful question, "The pink stuff?"

That's a reference to a typical antibiotic given to cats for a number of health problems. It is bright pink and administered with an eyedropper. To say that most cats do not like the "pink stuff," is something of a misnomer.

What cats don't like is being physically restrained while their mouths are pried open and an unwanted liquid is squirted down their throats. Think about that for a minute and you might realize you wouldn't like it either.

There have been great advances in methods of delivery for veterinary medications. When I had a cat suffering from high blood pressure, her medication was a topical cream applied to the inside of the earflap for absorption.

Some medications come as powders that can be hidden effectively in wet food, or even as flavored chews that are sufficiently tasty to cats to be seen as "treats." There is no need to hold down an angry, squirming cat while trying to get him to swallow liquid or a pill.

When pills and liquids are necessary, I won't lie to you. It can be "game on," with the cat holding a distinct advantage. Never underestimate the level of a cat's determination *not* to do something.

Don't think for a minute that you can hide a pill in a cat's food! Your pet will eat the food and you'll find the pill in pristine condition in the bottom of the bowl.

If you have to give your cat a pill, I recommend a direct, sure and fast approach. Gentle take hold of the cat's head from above. Use the index finger of your free hand to open the cat's mouth.

Put the pill as far back in the throat as you can. Gently hold the cat's mouth closed and try stroking your pet's throat to encourage swallowing. Vets have devices called pill "guns" that help to position the pill in the back of the mouth, but I've never been very good with them.

My theory is that the less fuss you make about it all, and the less chance you give the cat to run the show, the more successful you will be. Many people recommend wrapping your pet in a towel first, but I think that just sends the message, "We're getting ready to do something you won't like."

I have found that the same method works well with liquid medication, but I do not like to use the droppers that come with these preparations. I ask for an empty syringe with a mark to indicate dosage.

With the syringe, you benefit from a little more forceful "squirting" of the liquid that further encourages the cat to swallow. If the medicine in question is indeed the "pink stuff," expect your cat to have a little pink fur for a few days (and if I were you, I wouldn't wear white while dispensing the meds).

For any other kind of medications that might have to be administered in the home setting, rely on your vet's advice and ask for a demonstration. I have even given my pets subcutaneous fluid IVs at home. With proper instruction, any home treatment is possible.

Chapter 6 – Pet Insurance and Planning Ahead

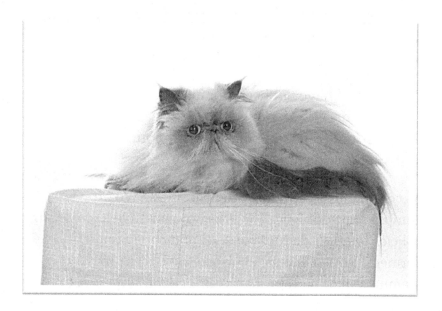

Pet insurance is a relatively new option and one about which owners have many questions. Advances in health care procedures for companion animals have substantially improved the lives of our beloved cats and dogs and extended their life expectancy in fantastic ways, but few if any of these procedures are inexpensive.

Is pet insurance worth the expense? Just as is the case with health insurance for humans, you must understand the reasoning behind paying for a policy.

Insurance is intended to help address unexpected large expenses that would represent a serious financial strain if paid out of pocket.

In survey results, significant numbers of pet owners admit they would spend any amount of money to save their pet's life. I have, on more than one occasion, gone into debt to pay for medical treatment for one of my cats.

Thankfully, I have not been put in a position to make an end-of-life decision for one of my pets based on financial hardship, but countless pet owners are put in this horrible position every day.

As companies offering health insurance have grown in number and sophistication, it is now possible to customize policies to select deductible level and copay options (termed "agreed excess levels" in the UK) to arrive at premiums that both protect your pet and fit into your budget.

Having an insurance policy will also broaden your options for treatment should your pet require the services of a specialist. In my case, one of my pets needed radiation treatment for an oral cancer. I borrowed the money, and spent the next four years paying his bills.

Do understand, however, that pet insurance reimbursement works a little differently than the regularly accepted human model:

- You pay the vet directly.
- You are responsible for filing the claim.

- You receive the reimbursement directly.

The reimbursement will include eligible expenses minus the level of your deductible and copy according to the set limits of the policy.

A comprehensive insurance policy for a cat including coverage for accidents, illnesses, and some hereditary conditions with an option for chronic condition coverage can be purchased for $15 - $25 / £9.75 - £16.25 per month depending on the deductible chosen.

Typically such policies carry up to $14,000 / £9,100 a year in benefits and are renewable on an annual basis.

Ask plenty of questions to determine the best company and plan for your needs:

- Can you go to your regular vet, or do you have to go to a vet assigned by the pet insurance company?

- What does the insurance plan cover? Does it cover annual exams? Surgeries? Emergency illness and injury?

- Does coverage begin immediately?

- Are pre–existing conditions covered? In addition, if your cat develops a health issue and you later have to renew the policy, is that condition covered when you renew your policy?

- Is medication covered?

- Do you have to have pre–authorization before your pet receives treatment? What happens if your cat has the treatment without pre–authorization?

- Does the insurance policy cover dental issues and chronic health problems?

- Is there a lifetime maximum benefit amount? If so, how much is that amount? A benefit plan with a lifetime maximum of only a few hundred dollars surely will not suffice!

- Is there an amount that you have to pay before the insurance pays out?

Take the time to research your pet insurance options. Compare the different plans available, what each covers, and the cost before making the decision on which is best for you and your pet.

Pet insurance may not be the answer for everyone. While it may not be a feasible option for you, consider having a backup plan, just in case your cat requires emergency care or you run into unexpected veterinarian costs.

A simple way to prepare for an emergency is to start a veterinary fund for your Himmie. Decide to put a certain amount of money aside each week, each month, or each pay–check to use in the case of an emergency. Think about the potential financial costs of veterinary care and plan for how you will pay for it now instead of waiting until something happens.

Companies in the United States offering pet insurance include:

Healthy Paws
HealthyPawsPetInsurance.com

PetPlan
GoPetPlan.com

Embrace
EmbracePetInsurance.com

Trupanion
Trupanion.com

Pets Best
PetsBest.com

Pet Premium
Enroll.PetPremium.com

The ASPCA
ASPCAPetInsurance.com

PetInsurance
PetInsurance.com

Pet First
PetFirst.com

24PetWatch
24PetWatch.com

Pet insurance companies in the United Kingdom include:

DirectLine
Directline.com/pet-insurance

VetsMediCover
Vetsmedicover.co.uk

PetPlan
Petplan.co.uk

Churchill
Churchill.com/pet-insurance

Animal Friends
Animalfriends.org.uk

Healthy Pets
Healthy-pets.co.uk

For a comprehensive comparison of policies see:
Money.co.uk/pet-insurance.htm.

Please note that all companies and links were active at the time of this writing in early 2014, but like all Internet content are subject to change. Since pet insurance is growing rapidly in popularity, use the search engine of your choice to look for additional coverage options. Note that the vast majority of sites allow visitors to obtain an estimate price quote online.

Planning for the Unexpected

If something happens to you, you want to know that your cat and any other pets will be properly cared for and loved. Some cell phones allow you to input an ICE (In Case of Emergency) number with notes. If your cell phone has such an option, use it. If it does not, write the following information on a piece of a paper and put it in your wallet with your driver's license:

- The names of each of your pets, including your cat.

- The names and phone numbers of family members or friends who have agreed to temporarily care for your pets in an emergency.

- The name and phone number of your veterinarian.

Be sure to also talk with your neighbors, letting them know how many pets you have and the type of pets. That way, if something happens to you, they can alert the authorities, ensuring your pets do not linger for days before they are found.

If you fail to do that and something happens to you, someone will find your cat and any other pets and will need to know what to do to ensure that they are cared for. It is a good idea in the case of an emergency, to ask several friends or family members to be responsible for taking care of your pets should something happen to you.

Prepare instructions for the intended guardians, providing amended instructions as necessary. Also, be sure to provide each individual with a key to your home (remember to inform your home insurance company so that this does not affect your coverage). Instructions should include:

- The name and phone numbers of each individual who agreed to take care of your cat and other pets.

- Your pet's diet and feeding schedule.

- The name and phone number of your veterinarian.

- Any health problems and medications your cat may take on a daily basis, including dosage instructions, instructions on how to give the medicine, and where the medicine is kept.

Put as much information as necessary to ensure the guardians can provide the same level of care to which your cat is accustomed.

Chapter 7 – To Breed or Not To Breed

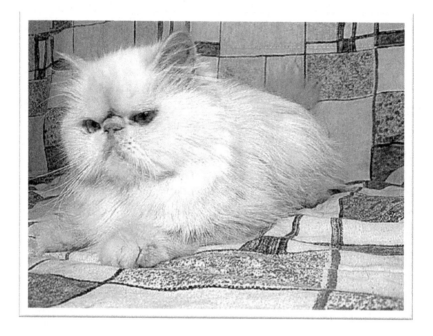

Over the years, I have been involved with the breeding of cats. I loved and enjoyed the experience, but I urge you to really think before taking that step. I have seen far too many cases of well-intentioned, enthusiastic people who start a cattery only to experience failure because they weren't truly prepared.

In these cases, the ones who suffer the most are the cats. That is the thing we all want to avoid, and what is always the most heartbreaking for the would-be cat breeder.

There's a terrific amount of guilt in the aftermath of a failed breeding operation.

No matter how rewarding you think the project might be, and I assure you can be, it's important that you consider the implications of running a cattery for both you and your family. For this reason, there are a number of things I'd like to suggest that you contemplate fully.

The decision to become a breeder of Himalayan cats or any other type of cat is one of those choices that may well *sound* better in theory than it plays out to be in reality. If you are considering becoming a breeder, understand from the beginning that you are not contemplating a mere hobby.

Dedicated breeders live and breathe the world of their cats. They share their lives with their cats, or, to put a finer point on it, order their lives according to the needs of their cats.

Also, do not think that becoming a cat breeder is a way to make money. If you have just paid a handsome price for a purebred Himalayan you may well snort at this assertion in disbelief. Yes, purebred kittens command high prices, but ask any breeder what happens to that money as soon as it comes into their hands.

Their answer will be a firm assurance that the amount goes right back out the door — to pay for vet bills, or cat food, or an addition on the house for the cats or any one of a hundred other cattery related expenses. Breeders who are honest will admit that in a good year, they break even.

There is only one reason to become involved in breeding cats — *love of the breed.*

Questions to Ask Yourself

If you are thinking about becoming a breeder, you need to immerse yourself in the culture of the cat fancy. Attend cat shows and make contact with existing breeders.

When you understand more about cat shows, you'll know that the event itself is not the place to try to have a discussion with a breeder. Instead, use these venues to collect business cards and to see examples of the breed in which you're interested.

Look for local Himalayan clubs to join, and find online discussion forums to learn more from working breeders.

Let me interject a word about forum etiquette. Never just jump into discussions as a "newbie." Spend a few weeks learning the culture of the forum before you post. It is far too easy to give offense without realizing what you are doing.

There are numerous questions you must pose to yourself. The contacts you make and the discussions you have with people knowledgeable about Himalayans and the operation of a cattery will guide you in forming your answers. Be honest with yourself! This is just a short list of things to consider:

- Do you have the time, including nights, weekends, holidays, to devote to the needs of your animals?

- Are you willing to allow your schedule to be dominated — often at a moment's notice — by your cats?

- Are you prepared for the heartache when kittens don't live?

- Are you prepared to see the kittens you have raised go to new homes? No matter how well you screen the adoptive parents or how much money you charge, that is still going to be a painful good-bye.

- Can you cover the initial financial outlay to not only make physical changes to your home, but also to acquire either a high quality queen or a breeding pair?

- Do you live in a setting that is even appropriate for this kind of endeavor? Are there zoning considerations? Homeowners association regulations? Tax implications?

Above all, outline Plan B. Of course you want to go into your new venture with optimism and enthusiasm, but temper that with a healthy dose of realism.

Know what you will do if it all goes wrong. You are bringing living creatures into your care. If you can't sustain the operation of your cattery, what will happen to them?

Memberships

You will gain more information and education from seeking out and joining breed clubs and professional breeder organizations. While there may not be a specific group for every breed, start with a major parent organization like The International Cat Association.

Even if the breed in which you are interested does not have a breeder's association per se, membership in major governing groups will help you to make contact with established breeders and potentially develop a mentoring relationship.

Compiling Estimated Costs

It is almost impossible to know all the costs that might be involved for any one person in setting up a cattery. My best advice to you is to imagine every possible expense and plan for it. Some of the more obvious items on this list should be:

Reference Materials

You are going to need to know everything there is to know about the Himalayan breed and its genetics. You will need reference materials including subscriptions to feline publications.

Foundation Animals

If you cannot afford a breeding pair, you will at least need a quality queen or stud. You will then need to factor in the cost of pairing your animal with a suitable mate from another cattery.

Veterinary Care

This is obviously a major routine expense for normal health care, but factor in infant and maternal services. Discuss the potential for problem pregnancies with your vet and find out in advance what emergency procedures like C-sections might cost.

You will also have to pay for repeat testing for your queen or stud if they are to go "visit" another cattery. At minimum you will have to produce the results of a recent FELV/FIV test each time.

Equipment, Furniture, Toys

In looking at these expenses, make a complete sub-list and then multiply the costs for everything including, but not limited to: cages, travel crates, play pens, climbing trees, beds and toys.

You will likely be creating an entire cat "room," so think about any kind of furniture you will need or any physical changes to the room that may be required to prevent escapes and enhance its security.

Construction Costs

If you have to add a room on to your house, work with a contractor well in advance of ever purchasing your breeding stock. Everything must be in place before you acquire your cats. If construction costs are prohibitive, this factor alone could derail your plans.

Insurance Considerations

It is impossible to predict the insurance considerations for every individual circumstance. If you are planning to start a cattery, however, a visit with your insurance agent is a must.

You may have to increase your coverage limits or add policy amendments or "riders" to cover additional equipment or square footage and to allow for visitors to your premises.

It is possible that you will also require both liability and indemnity insurance. Work with your agent to determine the appropriate level of coverage for your circumstances and to gain an estimate of the additional premium costs.

Emergency Reserve

It's considered "best practice" to have a 3-6 month operating reserve in cash. This is especially crucial if you are put in a position to shut down your operation since you will still have to feed and care for your animals during the time you are placing them in new homes.

Do not proceed without this emergency reserve in place. It's simply not fair to the innocent animals which will be depending on you completely for their well-being.

Going Forward

I've tried to be constructive in laying out some of the challenges and tribulations that will lie ahead of you as I feel it is important to contemplate and reflect on these before taking that big step.

I have seen too many cases of people with the best of intention and enthusiasm start an enterprise only for it to fail due to lack of preparation and thought with the only ones suffering as a result being their cats.

No matter how rewarding you think it might be, it is important that you consider the implications on your lifestyle and that of your family.

If my comments and observations haven't deterred you, then I applaud and welcome you to a most wonderful and challenging pastime which provides so much love and joy. The thrill and sense of achievement you will get from breeding your own Himmie is one that I know you will cherish and treasure in the years to come.

Chapter 8 – Showing Himalayan Cats

People who breed Himalayan cats do so in part to showcase the excellence of their bloodlines, so in this regard, participating in showing is an aspect of their business operations. An impressive collection of awards lends a high degree of prestige to any cattery.

At the same time, however, these people are dedicated proponents of the breeds they cultivate. Remember, however, that if you have purchased a Himalayan from a breeder, you have probably bought a "pet quality" animal. Show quality exemplars of the breed are easily twice the cost.

If you have a show quality cat, there is nothing to keep you from joining the show circuit. The Himalayan Breed, with its easy going, adaptable personality and calm demeanor, does better than many breeds with the whole process.

This must be, however, something of a "joint" decision. You have to decide showing is something you want to do, and then you must judge your pet's suitability to be shown. I am a firm believer that no animal should be made absolutely miserable just to be on a quest for a ribbon.

My best advice to you is to attend cat shows for the purpose of watching and learning. I'm about to run down the basics for you, but you have to experience a show first hand to get even the vaguest sense of the world you're thinking about entering.

The World of the Cat Show

I'm getting ready to give you a lot of information about cat shows, but I want you to hear one thing loudly and clearly from the beginning. When you go to a cat show DO NOT TOUCH THE CATS.

Don't Touch

Yes, you will be in the presence of cats that are physically beautiful and the urge will be overwhelming. Beyond the fact that it's bad manners, you represent a danger to those cats — or more specifically whatever is living on your hands represents a danger.

We walk around with bacteria and viruses on our hands at all times. As already noted, many feline diseases are so contagious all the animals have to do is tap noses to be infected. They don't need our help spreading germs all over their bodies petting them.

And what is the first thing a cat does after a good petting? Licks every hair to get the human scent off. I'm not being facetious. Cats prefer to smell like cats. They like the petting just fine, but they will still groom to make themselves smell the way they think they should.

If you have germs all over your hands, and the cat then licks its fur, the potential for illness is enormous. This is the reason for the "don't touch" rule.

Being invited to touch a cat at a cat show is a huge compliment, one usually extended along with a jar of hand sanitizer. Don't even blink. Use the sanitizer. Do it for the cat.

Don't Help

The second rule after don't touch is don't help. The cry of "loose cat" is heard fairly often in these venues. When a cat makes a break for it, the appropriate thing to do is freeze and be quiet.

Under no circumstances should you join the chase. You'll just frighten the escapee more. If you see the cat, get the attention of the owner and quietly signal where the cat is located.

Get Out of the Way

One thing you do want to do at a cat show is get out of the way. Often you'll hear a rushing exhibitor yell, "Right of way!" That's your cue to yield!

For that matter, don't be surprised if an exhibitor stops talking with you mid-sentence and goes dashing off. When exhibitors are called to the ring, they have only a limited amount of time to get there or be disqualified.

Do not be put off or offended by these instances. Cat shows can be very hectic and chaotic events. Don't contribute to the chaos.

Look and Listen

Remember that you are there to learn. Don't just look at the cats. Observe what's going on. Write down things you want to investigate or questions you want to ask.

Especially when you're near the ring where the judging is going on, be quiet and listen. You'll learn a great deal from the comments the judges make in the ring, and you certainly do not want to distract the exhibitors or the cats.

Cat Show Basics

While this may be the most obvious of statements, a cat show is not a dog show. There are definite differences in how the two kinds of events are run.

For starters, cats are kept secured at all times. Show cats stay in their cages, which are often quite elaborately decorated to call attention to both the animal and the cattery.

This fact lends a festive air to the whole exhibit hall, but the cage rule is strictly a matter of security. The idea is to avoid the "loose cat" situation, although, as we've discussed, that still happens all too often.

A point that is difficult for newbies to grasp is that in terms of movement, cat shows are very, very slow. However, when something is happening, they turn hectic in a heartbeat — like the regular mad dashes to the show ring.

Cat shows include a class for household pets; dog shows do not. The pet category is responsible for attracting many young people to the cat fancy and is a highly popular part of any show.

Judges evaluate all animals by breed standards formalized by the various agencies responsible for hosting and governing shows. Most of these standards follow or closely resemble the one established by The International Cat Association, which I provide for you later in this chapter.

The various governing bodies for cat shows include:

- The International Cat Association
- Fédération Internationale Féline
- World Cat Federation
- Cat Fanciers Association

- Feline Federation Europe
- Australia Cat Federation
- American Association of Cat Enthusiasts
- American Cat Fanciers Association

Is Showing Right for You and Your Cat?

Before you make the decision to show the Himalayan, or any other breed for that matter, you have a lot of research to do — on the breed in general, on your cat specifically, on the cat fancy, and on cat shows.

You do not have to participate in the world of the cat fancy to share your life with a beautiful pedigree animal, nor do you have to raise pure bred cats to enjoy their company.

Breeding and showing are pastimes and avocations that should have no other goals but furthering the development of the breed and supporting the welfare of the cats.

Only move forward with showing your cat if you are positive it is the right move for you, but especially, if it is the right move for your cat. If your pet is going to be miserable at a cat show, don't do it. No ribbon is worth that.

TICA Himalayan Cat Show Standard

PERSIAN BREED GROUP (PS/HI/ES)

The Exotic Shorthair (ES) is the shorthair equivalent of the Persian and Himalayan breeds and is differentiated from the Persian and Himalayan by coat length ONLY. It is accepted in ALL colors. Its plush, dense coat and similar type give the breed a teddy bear-like appearance.

The Himalayan (HI) is a man-made hybrid breed identical to the Persian, but distinguished by the points on the cats' extremities (the facial mask, feet, ears, and tail) which results in a Persian-type cat with the coloring and deep blue eyes of the Siamese-patterned cat. The Persian (PS) has a long coat, flowing all over the body with a dense undercoat giving the coat full volume. The ruff should be immense.

All traditional, sepia and mink colors are accepted.

Head 35

Shape - 5
Ears - 5
Eyes - 10
Chin - 3
Nose -5
Profile - 5
Neck - 2

Body 35

Torso - 10
Feet and Legs - 5

Tail - 5
Boning - 10
Musculature - 5

Coat/Color/Pattern 20

Length/Texture - 10
Color/Pattern - 10

Other 10

Condition - 5
Balance - 5

CATEGORIES:

PS: Traditional, Sepia, and Mink.

HI: Pointed.

ES: All.

DIVISIONS: All.

COLOR: All.

PERMISSIBLE OUTCROSSES: None.

HEAD:

Shape: Round, broad, smooth domed, with great breadth. Should be medium to large in size and in proportion to body. Jaws broad and powerful with perfect tooth occlusion. Cheeks should be full and prominent. Overall sweet expression.

Ears: Small and round tipped, not unduly open base. Set wide apart, fitting into contour of head.

Eyes: Large, round, and full. Set level and far apart giving a sweet expression to the face, eye color has equal importance to size and shape.

PS/ES: Deep brilliant eye color preferred which conforms to coat color.

HI: Deepest blue preferred, but light to medium blue is acceptable.

Chin: Strong, full, well-developed, fitting into the face.

Nose: Almost as broad as long with open nostrils. Muzzle should be short, broad and full.

Profile: Short, snub-nose, definite break directly between eyes. Forehead, nose and chin in straight line.

Neck: Short, thick, and well-muscled.

BODY:

Torso: Cobby, firm, well-rounded mid-section, in proportion. Medium to large in size. Back short and level. The chest is to be deep; equally massive across the shoulders and rump with a short, well-rounded abdomen and ribs.

Legs: Large bones, well-developed and with firm musculature. In front view, the forelegs should be short and straight from breadth of chest adding to sturdy appearance, not to have a bull dog appearance. When viewed from the rear, the legs should be straight.

Feet: Round and large.

Tail: Short and straight. In proportion to body length.

Boning: Heavy, sturdy and in proportion.

Musculature: Firm and well-developed, not overly fat.

COAT/COLOR/PATTERN:

Length:

(PS/HI) Long all over the body. Full of life. Dense undercoat giving the coat full volume. Ruff should be immense.

Seasonal variations in coat shall be recognized.

Length: (ES) Short, but slightly longer than other shorthairs. Soft, dense, plush; standing away from body. Seasonal variation in coat and density should be recognized.

Color: (PS/ES) As described in TICA Color

Descriptions.

COLOR: (HI) Clear color preferred with subtle shading allowed. Allowance should be made for darker shaded areas on coats of mature cats. There must be a definite contrast between the body and point color. The points, comprising of the ears, legs, feet, tail, and mask, must show the basic color of the cat.

OTHER: Condition/Balance: Should reflect excellent health and robust power with good muscle tone, well-muscled, but not fat. All parts of the body should be in proportion to each other.

GENERAL DESCRIPTION: The ideal PS/HI/ES is a strong cat with excellent boning and musculature, a well-balanced cat, giving the impression of robust power. The face should be round with a sweet, pleasant expression and large, round expressive eyes. The cat should be well-balanced physically and temperamentally, gentle and amenable to handling.

ALLOWANCES: Consideration should be given to the fact that females will generally be smaller than males, but should be in proportion and balance for their size.

PENALIZE: Long or narrow head; long Roman nose; thin muzzle; mild overshot or undershot jaw; bite deformity. Missing canine teeth in whole adult cats.

ASYMMETRY: while nature never creates a perfectly symmetric structure, recognition should be given to any obviously asymmetric head structure, (i.e., crooked or off-center nose, mouth, etc.). Such asymmetry should be penalized according to severity. Ears that are large, pointed, slanting out from the head or set too close together. A narrow chest, or long back. Poor muscle tone. Poor coat condition. Slab flanks. Small or close-set eyes. Pale, weak eye color.

WITHHOLD ALL AWARDS (WW): Overall lack of merit. Lockets or buttons. Poor overall condition. Eye color other than blue in Himalayans.

DISQUALIFY (DQ): Kinked tail. Severe malocclusion or extremely asymmetric face structure; crossed, slanted or improperly focusing eyes. Severe overshot or undershot jaw.

Temperament must be unchallenging; any sign of definite challenge shall disqualify. The cat may exhibit fear, seek to flee, or generally complain aloud but may not threaten to harm. In accordance with Show Rules, ARTICLE SIXTEEN, the following shall be considered mandatory disqualifications: a cat that bites (216.9), a cat showing evidence of intent to deceive (216.10), adult whole male cats not having two descended testicles (216.11), cats with all or part of the tail missing , except as authorized by a Board approved standard (216.12.1), cats with more than five toes on each front foot and four toes on each back foot, unless proved the result of an injury or as authorized by a Board approved standard (216.12.2), visible or invisible tail faults if Board approved standard requires disqualification (216.12.4), crossed eyes if Board approved standard requires disqualification (216.12.5), total blindness (216.12.6), markedly smaller size, not in keeping with the breed (216.12.9), and depression of the sternum or unusually small diameter of the rib cage itself (216.12.11.1). See Show Rules, ARTICLE SIXTEEN for more comprehensive rules governing penalties and disqualifications.

Revised 05/01/04 Persian Breed Group Standard, 05/01/2004

Chapter 9 – Himalayan Cats Care Sheet

Price: $1000 / £650

Physical Characteristics

Size: medium cat

Build: cobby or stocky build

Weight: 7 – 12 lbs. / 3.17 – 5.44 kg

Coat: thick, long, and silky

Color: pointed variations including: seal, blue, chocolate, lilac, flame, tortie, and lynx

Lifespan: 10 – 18 years

Grooming

5 to 15 minutes combing daily, monthly baths and possibly professional grooming.

Personality

Even tempered, affectionate, playful, but calm and not prone to separation anxiety.

Food and Water for Adults

Dry Food – Give a quarter to half a cup per day or 2 to 4 ounces / 56.7 to 113 grams.

Wet food – Give approximately 5.5 ounces or 156 grams once to twice daily.

Provide a constant source of clean fresh water.

Litter Box

Texture of litter and type of box to the cat's preference, scooped daily and changed out completely 1-2 times per week.

Health Care

Initial spaying or neutering with regular program of vaccinations in consultation with a qualified veterinarian. General preventive health care including dental. A hardy breed but somewhat prone to eye and nose problems if their facial features at flattened. See the chapter on health for a discussion of potential genetic health issues.

Closing Thoughts

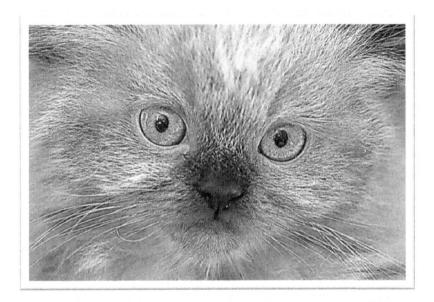

Hopefully you now understand that the Himmie is greater than the sum of its parts. They're a mellower version of the Siamese and a more active and involved version of the Persian. I can't think of any other sub-breed that so perfectly mixes the traits of its foundation breeds.

Thanks to the tolerance and patience of the Persian, the Himalayan is a highly cooperative cat that is perfectly willing to be groomed daily. In fact, a Himmie is willing to do most things so long as it gets to spend time with its human.

I especially like the quiet but involved presence of a Himalayan. Whether they're "helping" you read the paper, or instructing you on proper computer use from your lap, a Himmie is "there" in the nicest kind of way.

Don't be put off by all that lovely long fur. Yes, you'll need to put in 10-15 minutes of combing or brushing a day. And yes, you'll need to find a regular groomer, but Himalayans make all of that remarkably easy.

They're beautiful cats with beautiful dispositions, and are thus superb companions. As I've said before, I love all cats, but Himalayans are simple to love – in fact, impossible not to love.

If you are especially fond of the distinctive color pointing and blue eyes of the Siamese, the Himalayan will instantly capture your imagination. The combination of that classic oriental elegance with the softer, rounder curves and flowing fur of the Persian blends perfectly to create a unique breed – both in appearance and personality.

As a companion for singles or families, the Himmie is a stand out among felines, and one I highly recommend.

Relevant Websites

The Cat Fanciers Association, Inc.
www.cfainc.org

The Cat Site
www.thecatsite.com/a/himalayan-cats

The Cats of Australia
www.catsofaustralia.com/himalayan-cat-description.htm

Le Club Fur
A Brief History of Himalayan Cats
www.leclubfur.com/history.htm

The Atlantic Himalayan Club
www.himalayan.org/topcats.php

Himalayan Cats Online
www.himalayancatsonline.com

Catster - Himalayan Cat Info
www.catster.com/cat-breeds/Himalayan

Seattle Persian and Himalayan Rescue
www.seattlepersianrescue.com

The International Cat Association
www.tica.org/public/breeds/hi/intro.php

Kings of Siam
www.kingsofsiam.com/Himalayan.html

The Himalayan Cat
www.breeding-cats.com/himalayan-cat.html

Cat Care Zone
www.catcarezone.com/himalayan-cat-care

Meowmeister
www.meowmeister.com/himalayancats.aspx

Pawnation
www.pawnation.com/cats/breeds/himalayan

Shopping

www.PamperedCatShop.com

www.PamperedCatShop.co.uk

Frequently Asked Questions

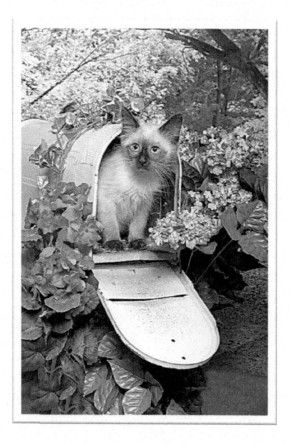

While I recommend that you read the entire text to get a good sense of life with a Himalayan, for those of you who like to get a "quick start" on a subject, these are some of the most frequently asked questions I encounter about this breed.

What should I look for in selecting a Himalayan kitten?

Generally kittens that are offered for adoption are at least 12 weeks of age. They should be happy and interested, with only a little initial shyness. There should be no discharge from the eyes and ears, and the ears should be clean with no odor.

Healthy kittens have soft, shiny fur that is thick and intact with no thin or bald spots. The body should feel solid and healthy, not bony. Good hydration should be evident in the gums, which should be pink and moist.

What's the best way to find a good breeder?

One of the best ways to get in touch with high-quality breeders is to attend cat shows. Catteries exhibit their finest animals at these venues and, while you cannot adopt on the spot, you can collect business cards.

Are Himalayan kittens born with long hair?

Himalayan kittens are fluffy rather than longhaired. Think of them as adorable little powder puffs.

Do Himalayans need any kind of special diet?

Any cat may need a special diet to help in the management of a health condition, but most cats, including Himalayans, thrive on a balanced and varied diet of high-quality wet and dry foods.

How much grooming is required for a Himalayan cat?

On a daily basis, 5-15 minutes of combing and brushing should prevent any matting and tangling in a Himalayan's coat. The cat will need to be bathed periodically, most likely by a professional groomer.

What equipment is needed for grooming?

The best implement for the Himalayan coat is a metal comb with alternating short and long teeth. Brushes can be used, but only with caution since they may contribute to tangling and matting. Consult with your breeder or groomer before buying a brush.

At what age should I begin to groom my Himalayan?

The sooner a cat becomes accustomed to daily grooming, the better. If you buy your Himalayan from a reputable breeder, the kitten should already be used to daily combing. Replicate the existing routine as closely as possible.

Will my Himalayan shed more seasonally?

Longhaired cats shed more in the summer months. Starting in the spring, you'll see an increased need for daily combing to stay ahead of the shedding and to prevent mats and tangles.

Is there any difference in temperament and adaptability in a male or female Himalayan?

The gender question really isn't a valid concern. All cats are individuals with unique personalities. Cats, like people, develop in response to their life experiences.

I've had cats of many breeds of both genders. I've rarely found gender to be an indicator of personality, and it is certainly not an issue with Himalayans. All are well mannered, sweet and agreeable.

Is there a problem with male Himalayans spraying?

I have never had an issue with male cats of any breed spraying, regardless of their intact or altered status. The behavior is even less likely in neutered males.

The neutering surgery is performed before six months of age. At that stage, the cats are just too young to start spraying.

Female cats can spray as well, although they do so only rarely. I think it's fair to say that well cared for, happy, healthy cats don't display problem behavior of any kind, including spraying.

The spraying stereotype is, in my opinion, unfairly applied to male cats. If it does happen, it likely indicates a cat that is either unhappy or physically ill.

Appendix 1 – Himalayan Cat Breeders List

United States

Beaukit Cattery
Barbara and Larry Bouchelle
Phone: 972-247-2147
Email: bouchel@sbcglobal.net
www.beaukit.com

By Heavenly
Brenda Morton
4697 Morton Road
Sutton, WV, 26601
Phone: 304-619-1429
Email: brenda59@mtn-air.net
www.heavensentpersians.com

Catortionist
Central New Jersey
Email: info@catortionist.com
www.catortionist.com

Cherishabuls
Email: cathy@cherishabuls.com
www.cherishabuls.com

Cuddle Paws
Debbie Evans
Bloomsburg, Pennsylvania
Email: duke1321@ptd.net
www.cuddlepaws.com

DiRose Cattery
Jacksonville, Florida
Email: himis@di-rose.com
www.di-rose.com

KaristaKats
Joan Donahue-Ulmer
Califon, New Jersey
Phone: 908-832-9188
Email: karistakats@comcast.net
www.karistakats.com

Karkens Cattery
Fairless Hills, Pennsylvania
Phone: 215-945-2775
www.karkenscattery.com

Meow House
Phone: 214-264-7261
Email: shannon@meowhousekittens.com
www.meowhousekittens.com

Napa Valley Persians
Gina Imrie
Phone: 707-287-2958
Email: ginadware@aol.com www.napavalleypersians.com

PuffStuff Cattery
Dr. Konstantin E. Voronin,
Dr. Larisa M. Voronin
Mt. Pleasant, SC, USA
Phone: 843-856-2852
E-mail: puffstuffcats@hotmail.com
www.puffstuffcats.com

Purrpalls
P.O. Box 3976
Citrus Heights, CA 95611-3976
www.purrpals.info

Rarebreed Cattery
Email: Amber@RarebreedCattery.com
www.rarebreedcattery.com

Sejumay
Email: debbie@sejumay.com
www.sejumay.com

Victorian Gardens Cattery
Susan Youngman
PO Box 264
Hamilton, NC 27840
Phone: 252-628-9104
www.victoriangardenscattery.com

Windy Valley Persians
Murrieta, California
Email: peekaboopersians@aol.com
www.peekaboopersians.com

Winnplace Cattery
Phone: 239-810-0066
Email: WinnnplaceCattery@aol.com
www.winnplacecattery.com

Vanleigh Persians
Email: vanleigh@bellsouth.net
www.vanleighpersians.com

United Kingdom

Ashaneeka Persians
www.ashaneeka-persians.co.uk

Shakira Persians
www.shakirah.com

Riascatz
Email: marie.hill@yahoo.co.uk
www.riascatzpersians.com

Canada

Avandel
www3.sympatico.ca/avandel

Koodos Himalayans
www.geocities.com/kudoscats

Ocean Purrls Persians
www.freewebs.com/oceanpurrlscattery

France

Devalpierre
www.devalpierre.com

Italy

Almigry
www.almigry.com

Appendix 2 – Toxic Plants List

The following is a fairly comprehensive though not exhaustive list but please check with your breeder or veterinarian for dangerous plants and flowers in your area.

Almond (pits)

Aloe Vera

Alocasia

Amaryllis

American Yew

Apple (seeds)

Apple Leaf Croton

Apricot (pits)

Arrowgrass

Asparagus Fern

Autumn Crocus

Avocado (fruit and pit)

Azalea Baby's Breath

Baneberry

Bayonet

Beargrass

Beech

Belladonna

Bird of Paradise

Bittersweet

Black-eyed Susan

Black Locust

Bleeding Heart

Bloodroot

Bluebonnet

Box

Boxwood

Branching Ivy

Buckeyes

Buddhist Pine

Burning Bush

Buttercup Cactus

Candelabra

Caladium

Calla Lily

Castor Bean

Ceriman

Charming Dieffenbachia

Cherry (pits, seeds, leaves)

Cherry Laurel

Chinaberry

Chinese Evergreen

Christmas Rose

Chrysanthemum

Cineria

Clematis

Cordatum

Coriaria

Cornflower

Corn Plant

Cornstalk Plant

Croton

Corydalis

Crocus, Autumn

Crown of Thorns

Cuban Laurel

Cutleaf Philodendron

Cycads

Cyclamen

Daffodil

Daphne	English Yew
Datura	Eucalyptus
Deadly Nightshade	Euonymus
Death Camas	Evergreen Ferns
Devil's Ivy	Fiddle-leaf Fig
Delphinium	Florida Beauty
Decentrea	Flax
Dieffenbachia	Four O'Clock
Dracaena Palm	Foxglove
Dragon Tree	Fruit Salad Plant
Dumb Cane	Geranium
Easter Lily	German Ivy
Eggplant	Giant Dumb Cane
Elaine	Glacier Ivy
Elderberry	Golden Chain
Elephant Ear	Gold Dieffenbachia
Emerald Feather	Gold Dust Dracaena
English Ivy	Golden Glow

Golden Pothos	Iris
Gopher Purge	Iris Ivy
Hahn's Self-Branching Ivy	Jack in the Pulpit
Heartland Philodendron	Janet Craig Dracaena
Hellebore	Japanese Show Lily
Hemlock, Poison	Java Beans
Hemlock, Water	Jessamine
Henbane	Jerusalem Cherry
Holly	Jimson Weed
Horsebeans	Jonquil
Horsebrush	Jungle Trumpets
Hellebore	Kalanchoe
Horse Chestnuts	Lacy Tree Philodendron
Hurricane Plant	Lantana
Hyacinth	Larkspur
Hydrangea	Laurel
Indian Rubber Plant	Lily
Indian Tobacco	Lily Spider

Lily of the Valley	Narcissus
Locoweed	Needlepoint Ivy
Lupine	Nephytis
Madagascar Dragon Tree	Nightshade Oleander
Marble Queen	Onion
Marigold	Oriental Lily
Marijuana	Peace Lily
Mescal Bean	Peach (pits and leaves)
Mexican Breadfruit	Pencil Cactus
Miniature Croton	Peony
Mistletoe	Periwinkle
Mock Orange	Philodendron
Monkshood	Pimpernel
Moonseed	Plumosa Fern
Morning Glory	Poinciana
Mother-in-Law's Tongue	Poinsettia (low toxicity)
Mountain Laurel	Poison Hemlock
Mushrooms	Poison Ivy

Poison Oak	Satin Pathos
Pokeweed	Schefflera
Poppy	Scotch Broom
Potato	Silver Pothos
Pothos	Skunk Cabbage
Precatory Bean	Snowdrops
Primrose	Snow on the Mountain
Privet, Common	Spotted Dumb Cane
Red Emerald	Staggerweed
Red Princess	Star of Bethlehem
Red-Margined Dracaena	String of Pearls
Rhododendron	Striped Dracaena
Rhubarb	Sweetheart Ivy
Ribbon Plan	Sweetpea
Rosemary Pea	Swiss Cheese plant
Rubber Plant	Tansy Mustard
Saddle Leaf Philodendron	Taro Vine
Sago Palm	Tiger Lily

Tobacco

Tomato Plant (green fruit,
stem, leaves)

Tree Philodendron

Tropic Snow
Dieffenbachia

Tulip

Tung Tree

Virginia Creeper

Water Hemlock

Weeping Fig

Wild Call

Western Yew

Wisteria Yews

Yew, American

Yew, English

Yew, Western

Yew, Wisteria

Source: The Cat Fancier's Association,
CFA.org/CatCare/HouseholdHazards/ToxicPlants.aspx

Glossary

A

Ailurophile – One who loves and is actively involved with cats. Also a committed member of the cat fancy.

Ailurophobe – Any person who harbors a dislike of cats or who has a fear of cats. This can be in response to a bad experience, a simple expression of preference, or an actual phobia.

Allergen – The primary allergen in cats is the protein Fel d 1, which is produced by the animal's saliva and sebaceous glands. In people with sensitivity, Fel d 1 triggers a pronounced allergic reaction.

Allergy – An allergy is a pronounced sensitivity to an environmental agent that triggers a cascade of responses in a sensitive person including, but not limited to, sneezing, watering eyes, itching and skin rashes.

Alter – An accepted term indicating that a cat or dog has been neutered or spayed and thus made incapable of reproduction. A similar, colloquial term frequently used with the same meaning is "fixed".

B

Bloodline – In pedigreed cats, the bloodline is the animal's verifiable line of descent. It is used for the purposes of establishing pedigree.

Breed Standard – Feline governing organizations publish established sets of standards outline the points considered necessary for an individual animal to be regarded as a perfect example of any given breed. The standards are used for the purpose of judging at cat shows.

Breed – Any group of cats with a defined set of physical characteristics that are reliably passed on to subsequent generations and that distinguish them from other types of cats is said to be a distinct "breed".

Breeder - A breeder is a person who works with male and female cats of a particular breed, pairing the animals to produce offspring that exhibit exceptionally high quality according to the accepted standards for the type of cat in question.

Breeding - In the sense of an organized promulgation of a breed within the cat fancy, breeding is the process whereby sires and dams are paired with an eye toward the superior quality of their offspring.

Breeding Program – A breeding program is an organized effort to selectively breed superior individuals of any type of cat for the express purpose of producing offspring of exceptional quality.

Breeding Quality – A cat is said to be of breeding quality when it exhibits sufficiently superior traits according to the accepted breed standard to be regarded as suitable for participation in an organized breeding program.

Breed True – When cats of the same breed pass on an identifiable set of physical characteristics from one generation to the next, those traits are said to "breed true". These might include such things as coat color or type, eye color, or physical conformation.

C

Carpal Pads - A cat's carpal pads are found on the animal's front legs at the "wrists". These pads serve to provide additional traction to the animal when walking.

Castrate – Castration is the medical procedure for the removal of a male cat's testicles to render the animal incapable of reproduction.

Caterwaul - A caterwaul is a high-pitched and strident feline vocalization that is discordant and unpleasant.

Cat Fancy – The "cat fancy" is comprised of those individuals actively interested in breeding, showing, and even simply appreciating cats of various breeds and types as well as the registered associations and clubs to which they belong.

Catnip – Catnip is a perennial herb in the mint family. Its scientific name is *Nepeta cataria*. Many cats are strongly attracted to catnip and exhibit mild intoxication upon contact with it. Kittens cannot experience this response, however, until they are at least 6-9 months of age.

Cattery – A cattery is any establishment where cats are housed, usually as part of an organized program of breeding.

Certified Pedigree – Certified pedigrees are issued by feline registering associations and are a validation of an individual animal's genetic authenticity as a prime example of a given breed.

Clowder – Clowder is a collective name indicating a group of cats gathered in one place at one time.

Coat – Coat is the accepted term used in reference to a cat's fur. The major qualifiers in this regard are long and shorthaired.

Crate – Any small container that can be securely locked and that is used to temporarily confine a cat or other companion animal for the purposes of safe transport is referred to as a "crate".

Crepuscular – Animals that exhibit crepuscular behavior are most active at dawn and dusk, which is the accurate term for the most active periods in a cat's day. It is not correct to say that these animals are nocturnal, even though they do possess excellent low light vision.

Crossbred – Any cat that is the product of a mating between a dam and a sire of different breeds is crossbred. This may occur as an accident or as an intentional effort to create a new and distinct breed exhibiting desirable qualities of the two foundation breeds.

D

Dam – In a mating pair of cats, the female is often referred to as the "dam".

Dander – Dander refers to the small scales that are shed along with the hair of an animal that are often created by saliva that dried on the fur as a consequence of self-grooming. Dander plays a leading role in the triggering of allergic reactions in people with specific sensitivity. In cats, the presence of the protein Fel d 1 in the dander is mainly responsible for this reaction in humans.

Declawing – Declawing is an extremely controversial surgical procedure in which the last digit of the cat's toes are removed so that the animal is permanently deprived of its claws. In theory the procedure developed as an anti-scratching measure, but it is now seen as excessive and cruel and is illegal in Europe and many parts of the United States.

Desex – "Desexing" is an accepted term to describe the procedures, either spaying or neutering, whereby animals are deprived of their ability to reproduce.

Domesticated – Domesticated animals are those creatures that, through long association, have come to be tame and to live in companionship with humans either to work or to serve as companions.

E

Ear Mites – Ear mites are microscopic parasites often present in the ear canals of felines. They cause redness and irritation, leading to an accumulation of black, tarry debris and often secondary yeast infections. This is an extremely unpleasant infestation for the cat accompanied by extreme itching. It is detectable not only by the visible inflammation, but also by the presence of a strong and unpleasant odor.

Entire – Entire is a term used in the cat fancy to describe an animal that has not been spayed or neutered and therefore has an intact reproductive system.

Exhibitor – An exhibitor is an individual who participates in a cat show either with a cat he or she owns or as a representative of the owner.

F

Fel d 1 – The protein Fel d 1 can be found in the sebaceous glands and saliva of cats. It is responsible for causing an allergic reaction in humans who have a specific sensitivity to it. This reaction includes, but is not limited so, sneezing, watering eyes, nasal congestion and itching.

Feline - A feline is any animal that is a member of the family Felidae. This group includes "big" cats like lions, tigers, and jaguars, as well as domestic cats.

Fleas – Fleas are parasites of the order Siphonaptera that feed on the blood of the host animal they infest. These creatures do not have wings, but are well adapted to jump.

Flehmening/Flehmen Reaction – In cats, the Flehmen Reaction is often mistaken as a facial grimace indicating dislike. In reality, this "expression" during which the cat holds its mouth partially open is adopted for the express purpose of allowing air to pass over a special structure in the roof of the mouth just behind the upper front teeth called Jacobsen's Organ. The organ, which is two small holes, functions as a secondary set of nostrils giving the cat the ability to essentially "taste" a scent or odor.

G

Gene pool – The gene pool in any population of organisms refers to the collective genetic information of the group relative to its diversity and reproduction.

Genes – Genes are the distinct hereditary units responsible for specific characteristics passed down from one generation of organisms to another. Genes consist of a DNA sequence found at a specific location on a chromosome.

Genetic – The term genetics is used in reference to any inherited trait or characteristic identifiable from one generation to the next.

Genetically Linked Defects – Any specific health or physical problem passed from one generation to the next that is, in some way, negative, harmful, or potentially limiting in nature.

Genetics – Genetics is the scientific study of heredity.

Genotype – A genotype is the term referring to the genetic makeup of an organism or a group of organisms.

Groom – Grooming refers to the procedures and protocols involved in caring for the coat of a cat including, but not limited to brushing, combing, trimming or washing.

Guard Hair – Guard hairs are longer, coarser hairs that form the outer or top layer of the coat on some breeds of cat.

H

Heat – "Heat" is the commonly accepted term to designate when a female cat reaches the point in seasonal estrus when she is ready to be impregnated by a male.

Hereditary – Hereditary elements including traits, diseases, or conditions are genetically transmitted from parents to their offspring.

Histamine - Histamines are physiologically active amines present in plant and animal tissue that are released from musk cells as part of an allergic reaction.

Hock – In anatomical nomenclature, a hock is that part of a cat's hind leg we would describe as the animal's "ankle".

Housetraining – Housetraining or housebreaking is the process of training a cat to live cleanly in a home with humans utilizing a litter box or pan.

Humane Societies – Humane societies are, in a general sense, groups working to end animal suffering as a consequence of overt cruelty, impoverishment or similar circumstances. The umbrella organization in the United States is The Humane Society of the United States and in the United Kingdom it is Humane Society International.

I

Immunization – Immunization is the targeted use of of injections for the purpose of cultivating immunity against disease. The injections are also commonly called vaccinations.

Innate – When a quality, tendency or trait is said to be innate, it has been present since birth.

Inbreeding – The act of inbreeding occurs when two cats with a close filial relationship, like siblings, mate and produce offspring. Typically this results in genetic flaws that become more serious the deeper the inbreeding penetrates into the gene pool.

Instinct – Instincts are patterns of behavior that are innate and come in automatic response to triggering stimuli in the environment.

Intact - Animals with complete reproductive systems are said to be intact because they are still capable of producing offspring.

J

Jacobsen's Organ – In cats the Jacobsen's Organ is found just behind the upper front teeth on the roof of the mouth. It is comprised of two small openings that function as second nostrils that allow the cat to "taste" odors or scents.

K

Kindle – Kindle is a collective term that refers to a group of cats in one place at one time. Another word with the same meaning is "chowder".

Kitten – A cat is said to be a kitten when it is less than six months of age.

L

Lactation – Lactation is the physical process by which

mammary glands produce and secrete milk for the nourishment of young mammals.

Litter – Litter is the collective term for all kittens born at one time to a single mother. Typically this is 3-4, but some litters can be as large as 6-10 or even 12-14 in some breeds.

Litter Box – Litter boxes are really any container of any configuration that is used for the express purpose of providing an indoor cat with a sanitary location to urinate and defecate in a provided collecting material like clay gravel or fine clumping sand.

Longhair – Longhair is a descriptive term for the coat of a cat that is marked by flowing length of fur, plumed tails and neck ruffs.

M

Mites - Small arachnids (*Acarina*) are parasites that infest both animals and plants and are often found in the ear canals of felines.

Moggy – Moggy is a term in the United Kingdom for a mixed breed cat.

Muzzle – A cat's muzzle is that part of the head that projects forward and includes the mouth, jaws and nose. It may alternately be referred to as the snout.

N

Neuter – Neuter is a term that specifically refers to the castration of a male cat to prevent the animal from impregnating females.

Nictitating Membrane – The nictating membrane, or third eyelid, on a cat is an inner transparent eyelid that works to moisten and protect the eye.

Nocturnal – Animals that are nocturnal are most active during the night. This term is mistakenly applied to cats. Felines are actually crepuscular, meaning they are most active at dawn and dusk.

O

Odd-Eyed – When a cat is "odd-eyed" it has two eyes of different colors.

P

Papers – A cat's "papers" are the official documentation of the animal's registered pedigree verifying the authenticity of its lineage as part of a designated breed.

Pedigree - A pedigree is essentially a cat's family tree or genealogy set in writing and covering three or more generations. The record is used to clearly establish the animal's genetic authenticity within a specific breed.

Pet Quality – Purebred cats that are designated to be "pet quality" have some physical characteristic or characteristics that diverge sufficiently from the accepted standard for the breed that they are not considered candidates to be shown or to be used in a breeding program.

Q

Queen – A female cat with an intact reproductive system is called a queen.

Quick – The quick of a cat's claw is the vascular "pink" just behind the white nail that will bleed profusely if it is accidentally clipped.

R

Rabies – Rabies is a highly infectious viral disease typically fatal to warm-blooded animals. It is transmitted by a bite from an infected individual and attacks the central nervous system causing severely aggressive behavior.

Registered Name - The registered name of a cat is the official name used by the registering agency on the animal's pedigree. The name is typically long and contains multiple references to the ancestry of the individual.

S

Scratching Post - A scratching "post" is any structure covered in carpet, rope, or similar material that has been constructed for the express purpose of allowing a domestic cat to sharpen and clean its claws without being destructive to household furnishings.

Shelter – A shelter is any local or regional organization that works to rescue and care for stray, homeless animals with the end goal of placing them in permanent homes.

Show Quality – Show quality cats are individuals that meet the official breed standard for their type and are thus recognized as suitable to be exhibited in cat shows and to be used in breeding programs.

Sire – In a breeding pair of cats, the sire is the male member.

Spay – Spaying is the procedure whereby the ovaries of a female cat are removed to render the animal incapable of producing offspring.

Spray – Spraying is territorial behavior most typically present in male cats involving the emissions of a stream of pungent urine to serve as a territorial marker.

Stud – Studs are male cats that have intact testicles so that they are suitable to serve as half of a mating pair in a breeding program.

T

Tapetum Lucidum - The tapetum lucidum is the interior portion of the feline eye that is highly reflective and aids in night vision. This is the portion of the eye that glows in photographs taken with a flash.

V

Vaccine - A vaccine is a preparation of a weakened or dead pathogen like a bacterium or virus. The vaccine is used to stimulate antibody production for the purpose of creating immunity against disease.

W

Wean – Weaning is the point at which a mother cat breaks her kittens away from subsisting on the milk she produces so that they begin to draw their primary nutrition from solid food.

Whisker Pad - The whisker pad is the thickened area on either side of a cat's face where the animal's sensory whiskers are anchored.

Whole – A whole cat is an individual of either gender with a functioning reproductive system.

Reference

Berg, Linda. "The Himalayan Persian." The Cat Fanciers
Association.
www.cfa.org/Breeds/BreedsKthruR/Persian/PERHIMArticl
e(1999).aspx (Accessed February 2014).

Brearley, Joan McDonald. *All About Himalayan Cats*. TFH
Publications, 1990.

The Complete Cat Breed Book. DK. April 2013.

Helgren, J. Anne. *Encyclopedia of Cat Breeds*. Barron's
Educational Series, April 2013.

Helgren, J. Anne. *Himalayan Cats: Barron's Complete Pet
Owner's Manuals*. Barron's Educational Series; 2nd edition,
September 1, 2006.

McDonald, Coleman. *Guide to Owning a Himalayan Cat*. TFH
Publications, 1997.

Persian Breed Group Standards
www.tica.org/members/publications/standards/ps.pdf

Richards, James. ASPCA Complete Guide to Cats:
Everything You Need to Know About Choosing and Caring
for Your Pet. Chronicle Books. September, 1999.

Rixon, Angela. *The Illustrated Encyclopedia of Cat Breeds*.
Wellfleet Press, January 2011.

All Photographs : www.bigstockphoto.com

Cover Design:- Liliana Gonzalez Garcia, ipublicidades.com
(info@ipublicidades.com)

Index

A

adoption   14, 15, 16, 23, 27, 28, 78, 121

American Association of Cat Enthusiasts   106

American Cat Fanciers Association   106

Australia Cat Federation   106

B

behavior/behaviors   8,
17, 34, 36, 49, 66, 71, 72, 123, 139, 144, 147, 148

boarder   60

breeders   4, 15, 18, 21, 22, 79, 94, 95, 97, 121, 124

breeding   2,
3, 22, 93, 94, 96, 97, 98, 100, 106, 137, 138, 146, 147, 148

brushing   55, 56, 65, 74, 116, 122, 142

C

carnivores   37, 71

Cat Fanciers Association   4, 105, 117

cat shows   95, 102, 104, 105, 106, 121, 137, 147

cattery   13, 15, 16, 17, 19, 22, 25, 47, 93, 94, 95, 96, 97, 98, 99, 101, 105, 138

combing   8, 55, 113, 116, 122, 142

D

declawing	23, 140
diet/diets	25, 40, 42, 43, 59, 64, 79, 82, 92, 121
disease/diseases	19,
38, 57, 61, 78, 79, 80, 81, 103, 143, 147, 148	
distemper combo	77
dry food	37, 41, 114, 121

E

ears	1, 4, 6, 20, 50, 54, 56, 73, 80, 107, 109, 110, 111, 121
euthanasia	67, 68
expenses	26, 69, 86, 87, 94, 98
eyes	1, 4, 6, 9, 20, 33,
50, 54, 56, 73, 80, 107, 109, 111, 112, 116, 121, 136, 141, 146	

F

Fédération Internationale Féline	105
feed/feeding	14, 26, 34, 37, 42, 43, 92, 99, 141
Feline Federation Europe	106
feline leukemia	78
FELV/FIV	22, 98
fleas	16, 20, 141

G

genetic/genetics	6,
23, 33, 78, 79, 82, 97, 114, 139, 142, 144, 146	
grooming	2,
8, 9, 11, 12, 21, 26, 51, 52, 55, 57, 113, 122, 140, 142	

gums   73, 79, 81, 121

H

health problems   16, 37, 61, 83, 88, 92
houseplants   30, 31
human health considerations   28
hypertrophic cardiomyopathy   79

K

kitten 13, 14, 15, 16, 17, 19, 20, 21, 24, 25, 26, 28, 30, 31, 32, 33,
    43, 47, 77, 121, 122, 144
kittens   6, 13, 17, 18, 19, 22, 30, 81, 94, 96, 121, 138, 145, 148

L

litter box   17, 25, 35, 37, 43, 47, 65, 66, 74, 114, 143, 145

M

matting   65, 122
milk   40, 145, 148

N

neutered   8, 14, 22, 76, 123, 136, 141
neutering   22, 23, 76, 114, 123, 140
nose   6, 19, 54, 61, 72, 78, 80, 107, 109, 111, 114, 145
nostrils   20, 72, 109, 141, 144

W

CPSIA information can be obtained
at www.ICGtesting.com
Printed in the USA
LVOW13s0341210917
549487LV00024B/1216/P